The col

Israel Aszendorf

Translated and edited by Alexander Ashendorf

Printed by CreateSpace, an Amazon company.

ISBN – 13: 978-0692907399
10: 0692907394

Library of Congress Control number:2017910068
Alexander Ashendorf, Staten Island, NY

CreateSpace Independent Publishing Platform,
North Charleston, SC

Contact: alexashendorf@gmail.com

To

The memory of my father
Israel Aszendorf

Table of contents

The life and works of Israel Aszendorf, 1909-1956.

Born in Mielnitsa in Polish Galitsia (now in the Ukraine). Grew up in Lemberg/Lvov (Now Lviv) Studied in Hebrew school and later in a teachers' seminary. Started writing in his youth. Debuted with a poem in 1927, in *Unzer Hofenung* and in *Yungt-veker* (youth alarm), *Folkstzeitung* (people's newspaper) and *Literarishe Bleter* (Literary leaves) in Warsaw and Lemberg.

Israel Aszendorf (on left) with family in Poland before WW2

In the 1930's he was, along with Rachel Korn, S. Imber, Ber Horowitz and others, part of the *Tsushteyer* (contribution) group. He was secretary of YIVO and the Yiddish theater society in Lemberg, in 1937-39. He adapted two works of A. Goldfaden for the theater:

Bar Kokhba and 'Di Broder Zinger' (The brother singers) which played in Warsaw in 1938-39

Israel Aszendorf (fifth from left) and my mother Rachel (eight from left) next to Abraham Zack, Yitzhak Yanasovitch, Nahum Bomzeh and other fellow authors in Paris, early 50'.

From 1939 to 1945 he lived in the Soviet Union, mostly in Tashkent, (in today's Uzbekistan.) At one point worked as a medic. And some odd jobs, where he spent some of his time with the poet Naum Bomzeh. In 1945 returned to Poland where he found that his entire immediate family of five brothers a sister and mother, had perished in the Holocaust. Was active in reconstruction attempts of Jewish life in Poland after the war. Aided with the Jewish Theater in Lodz and wrote children's poems. In 1948 went to Paris, where he married and had a son. Was editor of the literary journal *Kiyum* (Existence). In 1951, he was given the Alexander Shapiro award for creativity for his '*King Saul'* which he shared with H. Leyvick. In 1952 received the *Yud Lamed Peretz prize from the 'Congress*

Culture' for the same work. In the early fifties he visited Israel and at one point was in negotiations with the national theater 'Habima' for featuring his play *King Saul* which had been translated to Hebrew. however, the Israeli cultural and theater establishments of the day did not look favorably on Yiddish as it was anathema to a new nation struggling to renew itself in Hebrew, and he felt that he was getting the cold shoulder. In 1953 he immigrated to Argentina where he worked as a teacher of Hebrew and Yiddish literature in a teachers' seminary, a collaborator in the *Yiddishe Tseitung, an*

Rachel and Israel Aszendorf (mom & dad). Paris, circa. 1951

inspector of Jewish schools, and was vice president of the Jewish writers' union in Buenos Aires. published in *'Tsukunft'* (Future), and *Yiddisher Kemfer* (Jewish fighter) in New York, and *Goldene Keit* (Golden Chain) in Tel-Aviv. Several of his poems were translated to Hebrew by Shimshon Meltzer, and one story of his: 'A relative' by Rachel Auerbach. Another story 'The strange story of Haim Haykel the cat' and the poem 'Dust' were translated to Spanish and appeared in print in Argentina. Many of his articles poems and stories have appeared in a multitude of Yiddish newspapers in Europe, Israel, Argentina Canada, South Africa and New-York.

Speaking at an award ceremony (probably) in Buenos Aires

Historical background

Secular Yiddish literature came into bloom with the works of Shalom Aleichem, Mendele moykher Sforim and Y.L. Peretz in the late 19th century. In their stories, they describe the transition of the

Jewish people in eastern Europe from poverty, religiosity and tradition, to immigration to better places and secularism – all influenced by the movements of the Jewish Enlightenment, Zionism, and by the Pogroms.

This literary movement was significant, until some years after the second world war.

With the destruction of a large population of Yiddish speakers in the holocaust, the survivors dying out, and most of the following generations abandoning Yiddish as their vernacular, the amount and quality of Jewish Literature, has shrunk tremendously.

In his poems stories and plays, Israel Aszendorf traces Jewish life in the early 20th century shtetl, all the way through the prewar socialist revolutionary zeal, WWII, the life of a displaced Jew in Europe, and then, the attempts to build a new life away from Europe in Argentina. Many stories are autobiographical at least to some degree, and as such, one could consider the total body of work as describing the zeitgeist of 'secular' Jewish life between the mid-twenties and early fifties of the twentieth century.

A task he did not accomplish was the writing and publication of his *King Solomon,* the third book in the trilogy of first three Hebrew kings, and also the publication of other plays, a children's story book, and other short stories. Which I, (his son Alexander) have gathered, translated and am bringing to print in this and sister volumes. Some of his work had been commented on and showcased mostly in the 1950's in the following publications:

Yiddisher Shriften. (Lodz) *Unzer vart* (Paris) *Yiddishe Tseitung* Buenos Aires) *Literarishe Bletter*. Kiyoom (Paris), *Argentiner Beymlech* (Buenos Aires) *Unzer Shtimeh* (Paris) Di Presse (Buenos Aires) *Lashon un Leben* (London) *Yiddisher Cultur*(New York) *Goldene Keyt* (Tel Aviv)*Der Morgen Journal*, *Der Shpigel* (Buenos Aires) *Keneder Odler* (Canada) *Unzer Gedank. La Vie Juive* (Paris) *Afrikaner Yiddisher Tseitung* (South Africa) *Comentario* (in Spanish) (Buenos Aires). His work had been commented on by the following colleagues and critics: Melekh Ravitch (My Lexicon)

The Yiddish Lexicon, Moshe Knapheiss, Y. Harn, R. Feder, Gabriel Weismann, Isaac Yanasovitch, Melech Tchemney, Mates Dytch, Abraham Zack, Dr. A. Mukdony, Dr. Shlomo Bikel, Y. Freilied, Yaakov Glatshtein, Yaakov Glantz, Abraham Shulman, Haim Leib Fooks, A. Domankevitch, Rachel Auerbach and Yaakov Botoshanski.

His main publications were:

In a great unknown city,	**Poem**	1932	In a groyseh fremdeh shtot
Monday Morning,	**Poems**	1937	Montik inderfri
Greetings from far,	**Poems**	1939	Grissen in der veit
Premonition and reality**,**	**Poems**	1941	Anung oon var (lost)
King Saul **,**	**Play**	1948	Der Meylekh Shaul
Woe and wander**,**	**Poems**	1950	Vey oon vander
Partners in fate**,**	**Stories**	1953	Shootafim foon goyral
King David,	**Play**	1956	Der Meylekh David
Last writings,	**Stories, plays,** and **poems** (Posthumously)	1958	Letsteh Shriften

The last five books on the list above, could be read in Yiddish on the internet archive (Open Library. Org) or the national Yiddish book center/ Spielberg Digital Yiddish Library, the top first three, as well as some other plays, poems and stories which are not available there, I plan to submit to them in the near future.

The first three publications, *'In a great Unknown city' 'Monday morning'* and *'Greeting from far',* contain poem written between the first and second world wars. They are the works of a poet deeply moved not only by the economic plight of his immediate family, but also of humanity at large: the factory worker and the common man. It was a time of revolutionary zeal, when in the depressed and war-ravaged Europe of the time, socialism and unionism had more of an appeal than they have today. Also, to be young and idealistic also meant, in many cases to be a socialist.

(My mother once told me that when he worked for his brother's business, he organized the workers and they declared a strike). His next book of poems, 'Woe and wander' (1950) seems more of a mature work and has more of an expanded subject matter. It contains poems from different periods i.e. early childhood and the holocaust, and some with a more of an abstract and/or lyrical tone, such as "Beards", "Letters" and "Dust". The book also has some of his earlier poems reworked and presented there.

King Saul and *King David*, are two plays about the first two kings of Israel, written as 'biblical poems'. As mentioned above, the third and final one in the trilogy was never written.

Partners in fate, contains 10 Stories. It introduces Israel Aszendorf's alter ego, David Farber. A peculiar exception in this book is the story *'The strange story of Haim Haykel the cat'* which unlike all other stories in this book, is of pure fantasy.

Last writings, is a posthumous compendium of stories, poems, one acts, and miniatures.

In his introduction to his 'Vey un Vander' (Woe and wander) He mentions that some works were lost during the war: the poem 'Uriel Acosta', 'I invite you to a mascaraed Ball' and the book 'Anung oon Var' (Premonition/news and reality) as well as many others.

"I invite you to a mascaraed ball had been found, but not so other ones.

I will be very happy to hear from anyone with possession or knowledge of a lost work. At the time of his death he was about to publish a book with ten one act plays, a children's story book, and as mentioned above, had plans for writing 'King Solomon', the third play in the trilogy of the kings. Additionally, his plan book shows many ideas for additional short stories. The material which had been published in newspapers at the time or remained unpublished, in family archives is being brought to print in this series.

Translator's note

It is more than sixty years since my father's untimely death in Argentina, and I am older now than my father ever was.

Until very recently, I didn't know any Yiddish and could not read any of his work. After my father's death my mother moved to Israel; Israel had adopted a newly refurbished Hebrew as its national language as both a practical and political necessity. Yiddish, Being a Germanic language, foreign in sound and bearing different cultural connotations, the Jewish immigrants from Arab countries would not speak it. Also, Yiddish met with the disfavor of the young country's leaders who associated it with an old image of an oppressed Diaspora Jew, and its study was suppressed. As for myself, I'd left Israel in the early 80's and came to the U.S. to start a new life. I had to concentrate on English, and so, I had to take the study of Yiddish later in life.

Of the total body of work there were translations of very few pieces into Hebrew Spanish and English, but the majority of the works have remained until now, mostly untouched. Since the end of the Second World War, secular Yiddish literature has been constantly reduced in numbers of both readers and literary works. By my reckoning Yiddish users today are of three types: the ultra-orthodox community, who is not the main customer of modern secular Yiddish writing,

Old, non-ultra-orthodox Jews who still remain since the 'old days' of the middle of the twentieth century, some isolated communities, and a younger generation where Yiddish has generated renewed interest. However, the recent small resurgence of Yiddish is not the same as having entire communities of millions of Jews using it as their vernacular; and so, with the destruction of European Jewry, their mass migration to the United States and Israel, and increased political freedom and prosperity, came more assimilation and abandonment of their roots. Some Jews call this process a second Holocaust, a cultural one...

These trends didn't bode well for my father's work being sought in its original form. With the continuation of the current trend and dwindling in the numbers of potential readers, chances are that my father's work would disappear, so I decided to undertake its translation.

There is a note at the end of his book 'King Saul' about books about to be published. It mentions '10 one act plays. Unfortunately all I could find were the eight plays presented here.

It goes without saying that with every translation there is a lot lost. With its own rich cultural heritage Yiddish has its own unique obstacles; many words and concepts are untranslatable and require footnotes. Connotations are lost, and terms of endearment that are so common in Yiddish do not have an English equivalent. The flavor and music of the language is lost... so a translator must take some poetic license and the work is to some extent recreated.

In the process of editing the material, I was faced with the dilemma of **what not to publish**. I decided, however, that since these books are not only the 'Collected works of...' but also 'In memory of...' I would include everything I had.

Readers familiar with the names of the biblical characters presented, will notice that I am using a spelling which is different. e.g. Avshalom rather than Absalom, or, Avner rather than Abner. This is consistent with the original Hebrew. Nevertheless, for reasons of expediency and reader comfort, I chose to leave 'Jerusalem' and 'Saul' the way they are known and used in English.

New-York, February 2018

My father and I on vacation. Argentina, 1955

*   *
*

King Saul

A Historical Tragedy

Originally published in Yiddish in Lodz, 1948

To the holly memory of my
mother Sloveh, my sister Bayleh,
my brothers Moshe, Uri, Yitzhak,
Moony and Hanna, who were killed,
by German murderers.

Dedication

Childhood images once more
I see before my eyes.
I'd thought: to my remembering
I long ago did close the door.
Childhood, it is true — forgot me;
But you — I shall always recall!

I met you every time
In old pages of the Torah
Escorting me upon the road
Back from school at night.
I was in bed already lying,
And thinking of you more.

I envied little David
How well he lobbed the stone,
And made the harp intone
Some pretty wondrous songs;
And from the book of psalms
I taught myself some more.

I was concerned for Samuel
For he reproved a king,
I saw Saul's beard in black
And David's beard — a blond
But Samuel's beard was stubby
Like a frozen icy poke.

Of Samuel — fear was lost
My love — had turned to David.
And Saul's fate had forever
With triumph's fire — burnt me
Therefore, with love, and dread
I put the book right in your hands.

Characters:

Samuel	the prophet
Saul	the King
Akhinoam	Saul's wife
Mother	Saul's
Yonatan	Saul's eldest son
Mikhal	Saul's daughter
David	her husband
Avner	Saul's chief of the army
Tirtsa	sorceress
Aviyah	her daughter
Armor bearer	Saul's
Messenger	David's

Elders, warriors, prophets, common Israelites, Philistines.
The events take place in Ramah, Gilgal, Giva'a, Ein-Dor, and mount Gilboa.
Time: 1010- 1030 BCE

First Act

Ramah: a square in front of Samuel's house, common people and elders.

Lament song of the men

In days of spring we sowed the land
Dew did come, and rain did pour;
From heaven climbed the sun
And shot its rays, as it arose.
From dark soil came the singing grain,
We harvested, we threshed and milled:
Great abundance, out of mount and vale —
And brought it home to barn and vault.
But our land an enemy attacked,

Robbed, laid waste and set aflame!
Oh, land, why didn't you rage
Against the plow — if you foresaw?
Oh heaven, with your dew, all came to bloom —
Why haven't you with sulfur had it soiled?
Why, oh wind, the seed you didn't carry off?
Why, oh hail, you did not strike the fields?
But rather let the grain rise high
And let our enemy — with it abscond?

Lament song of the women

In nights, in fervor — we conceived,
Bore children weak as hens:
Nursed them, lulled to sleep and watched,
With sickness and no food —
With life and death, for them we wrestled,
Until each one with fortune grew:
The virgins: pretty, slender, like the cedars
Strong and nimble were the boys.
Upon our land the enemy descended
Killed and raped, and made us slaves.
Oh think: why did we open for the seed?
We should have been as fruitless as a void!
Oh breast, you gave milk gladly — when
You should have been as hard as stone!
A curse should have befallen on our flesh,
That we forever barren be,
Than see our proud boys now enslaved,
Our daughters in the market sold as whores!

First man: Today it is a holiday in Israel, but no singing,
And no dancing and no laughter; only
Ashes on our heads and torn-up garments.

Second man: How much longer shall we grieve and cry?
Let's go to the prophet, to the prophet
Samuel.

Third man: The prophet is now old.

Forth man: And broken down with pain.

Second man: Then let him designate another,
To lead against our foe.

First man: Such as Gideon!

Third man: Such as Yiftah!

First man: The times of Judges are now done.
A hero used to lead the people,
And when he died, the people, then,
With no redeemer then remained.
Now we need a race of heroes:
When one is dead, his son will reign!
The people need a king!

(The word King has a magical effect over all)

Everybody: A king!

Voices: Let's go to Samuel!
To the prophet!
Let him give us a king!
A king!

(The crowd is agitated. All run to Samuel's house. The first elder blocks their way)

First elder: Not one more step — all halt!

A voice: What does the old man want?

First elder: You can't all come to him as one —
And speak to him, now can you?
Choose some, to speak on your behalf.

Voice: We need no one — but the elders,
Let the elders speak for us!

Voices: Let the elders go! The elders!

(Three elders step up in front of the crowd)

First elder: So shall it be, but first we should have counsel.
Go back, and wait for our answer.

(The crowd moves back and the three elders remain)

First elder: Remember, have no fear,
No childish stammering.
We're going now not only in our name:
From our mouths will speak our nation.

Second elder: I hope he doesn't think — we try to undermine him.
I hope he doesn't think — we do not trust him
Oh, he will be cross!

Third elder: People say: the prophet's hard and piercing eyes,
put your heart aflutter, and your knees,
they buckle under.

First elder: If you're already so afraid,
How will you face him later?
When we stand before him —
We have to be — not three, but one!
For our complaint is really single!
Give us a king, oh, prophet!

Second elder: Who shall it be, and from which tribe?

First elder: That person should be chosen by the prophet:
From which tribe should he come?
Clearly, from the largest one in Israel,
The most important — Judah is the one!

Second elder: Judah? I really think that he should come
From the glorious tribe of Aaron and
Moses — from the tribe of Levi.

First elder: As if it weren't enough, that
You control the heavens,
Now — you would also take the earth?
You've taken plenty — priest!

Third elder: From my tribe, someone already reigned,
Joseph the dreamer, back in Egypt.
If it's a king you want, then only from
Ephraim!

Second elder: He who lorded over strangers doesn't fit to
be our leader!

First elder: No more chatter! Here's the prophet!

(Enter Samuel)

Samuel: I had a wondrous reverie,

But sudden shouting from the street
Disturbed it — God appears only in peace…

First elder: And the people in a racket!

Samuel: (As if waking up from sleep)

What do you seek here, elders?
I see your faces cloudy;
About to bring the thunder — speak!

First elder: We're sent here by the people… envoys…

Samuel: I come myself to them when it is needed.

Second elder: Forgive us and the people, prophet…
Their suffering and bondage brought us here
and… their wish for freedom.

Third elder: You've known that for some time:
The Philistines put governors
In our towns, and take a toll
From our grain and cattle.
And more than that, they sack
Our cities and our farms.
They take our flocks of sheep and cows
They rob the barns and vineyards,
And desolate our fields and orchards.
Our graceful sons and daughters,
Sold as slaves and servants.

First elder: We would not be silent, for
Brave youth in Israel is aplenty.
Still, we have no weapons,
As the hated philistines forbid us to engage
In forging and in smithing.

Second elder: And lately, worse than that transpired:
They picked themselves a king:
King Akhish is very brave and daring!
Already managed to beat Sidon,
Who knows whether tomorrow or today
He won't attack us.

Samuel: God will guard you and protect you!

First elder: God has abandoned us,
The only one to save us,
Is a king,

Samuel: (surprised)
A king?

First elder: To unify the tribes —
Twelve tribes — to be as one.

Samuel: It's not the tribes that separate you
It's the idols!
And not a king — it ought to be
Which binds you, but one God.
No taxes to Akhish will hurt you
But the sacrifices to Dagon their Idol!

First elder: If the Philistines prove strong,
The people will respect their Idols,
But once they've lost — Israel will
Smash their bogus Gods to dust.
For who would serve a God that can't help out?

Samuel: Don't you know the conduct of a king?
He'll take your strong and handsome sons,
To plow and sow his fields and run before
His carriage for his honor.

Your noble daughters he will take
For servants, cooks and maids.
The finest fig and olive trees he'll give
To his ministers and kin.
And tithe your fields and cattle;
Your slaves, your camels, donkeys,
He'll burden with a yoke of endless toil.
To God you will be crying for salvation,
That he may free you from the yoke of kings
But God will turn away and not —
Protect you from your savior!

Second elder: The king will take our gardens and therefore
Those that are left he will protect from our foes.

Third elder: And when we win a battle, will share with us the spoils of war.
Some of us he'll take as servants,
But also turn some others
Into heroes and advisers.

Elders: Oh prophet! Give us a king, a king!

Samuel: It's true I've aged and can no longer come to
Distant towns and villages, and carry justice:
But my children, Joel and Aviah…

Second elder: They are judges, for domestic quarrels
Not for waging war against a stranger.

First elder: It would be much more painful for a father to
Discover, but a prophet — must know facts.
Your children strayed from righteousness,
They sell their justice for a bribe.

(The elders wait for Samuel's answer but he is silent. They become discouraged and they look at one another, lost, finally the prophet says:)

Samuel: You are now, my honored guests:
Off your feet my servants now
Will wash the dust: have some food,
Nourish your heart, and wait awhile
And I will hear what god commands.

(Exit the elders)

Like throwing rocks they threw at me
The grave misconduct of my sons
And I the father kept my silence.
That surely must be how Ali felt
Then, on the night, I came to him.
When God had summoned me three times.
How pale and lost was the old man!
Not his children would his place
With God inherit, but I — a stranger of a man.
Oh, fate ever recurring!

(Pause)

And now what should I do? What answer
Should I give the people and the elders?
If I won't find a man after my heart,
Will come — a charmer, a deceiver,
And while the crowd is hot, he will —
The royal crown put on his head.
Admit it Samuel — as painful as it is
Your time has passed. The people ought to have a second leader, one of a different sort.
If our enemy depends on power,

Then Israel too — should have a man of might.
To raise his sword against all enemies.
But I — must be the scabbard of that sword.
Outside the people wait; outside the elders wait,
Who should I choose, who should I, who?

(Suddenly he feels someone near him. he quickly turns about,
In front of him stands Saul)

Saul: Are you Samuel, Samuel the seer?

Samuel: I am Samuel, don't you recognize me?
For years I have been going
On the road from town to town
From one village to another
To make a law for Israel.

Saul: Forgive me holly man,
But he who has no quarrels
Doesn't know a judge

Samuel: Who are you then — which is your tribe?

Saul: A man remembers stately cedars
But who recalls the shrub and bush?
My name is Saul, and I am from
The tribe of Benjamin.

Samuel: What is the reason for your coming
to this place?

Saul: We lost our donkeys…

Samuel: Rest assured my son — they will be found.
And what's your trade in Benjamin?

Saul: I work the field with my oxen
And even though I have my grown children,
I live together with my parents.

Samuel: And do you walk among your people?

Saul: I'm strong and taller than the rest
Wherever I may be — they all can see me.
My strength does frighten all the people
(For all they see in human strength,
Is violence and murder.)
Therefore I stay close to my own.

Samuel: (to himself)

You have found favor in my eyes
You are a quiet humble man.
A man such as yourself,
Can loyal be and grateful,
And most importantly, obedient.

(Out loud)

Saul of Benjamin!
The elders now are resting in my home
Soon I will prepare for them a meal,
And you as well are welcome, us to join.

Saul: I would be choking on the food,
If I were sitting with the prophet
And the elders at one table.

Samuel: When eating with great people,
Bitter is the biting,
But son, you ought to learn

The bitter fare to swallow.

Saul: What am I, oh prophet? What is my import?
My tribe's the smallest in the land,
My household, smallest in the tribe.

Samuel: If your tribe has not been noticed by the people,
Let it now become the launching of its glory.
And if it's small — know this:
The number of the ruler's always smaller
Than the number of his subjects.

(Brings a jug of oil)

Come my son and bow your head,
I will anoint you for a king of Israel.

Saul: Anoint me for a king?
Is the prophet joking?

Samuel: God ordered me as follows:
As Saul protects and loves his kin,
I will now give to him a greater family to keep:
That of the people of Israel!

(He anoints Saul)

Hear me out, son of Kish:
God has picked you for a king
To lead his chosen people.
Until now, he never did divide his reign;
Moses never wore a crown
Joshua too did not receive it
None of the judges rose to kingdom.
I had warned the elders
Of the conduct of a king.
Now, son of Kish beware

In how you lead the people. Know this: as two men come to court,
Only one shall leave content;
The second will become your hater.
The fools will look at you dismissively,
Thinking a crown is all it takes to be a king
And they will praise you wickedly
For they will often want the crown
Not only as a cover for your head, but also
For their ugly deeds.

(Enter the elders)

First elder: Oh prophet! The people are restless,
We need an answer!

Samuel: Good, I have picked a king,
God had thus commanded me to say:
Do not reproof the elders
Don't pour on them your anger,
Not you, but I, have lost my favor,
And for Israel I'll pick a king.
I did for you now, choose that man.

Elders: Was the king already chosen?

Samuel: The man is here right in this room.

(The elders look around in confusion: which one of them was chosen? They do not notice Saul, who is standing in the corner.)

Elders: And which one of us is chosen?

Samuel: (pointing at Saul)
There he is, the man in the corner!

(The elders notice Saul)

Second elder: And who is that unknown man?

Third elder: And what's his origin and tribe?

Samuel: His name is Saul.

First elder: And from which tribe?

Saul: The son of Kish… from Giva'a… Benjamin...

Firs elder: Is the prophet being flippant?

Second elder: Or is Israel like the mistress of the hill
That all did rape?

Samuel: Do you elders mean to buck me?

Third elder: Who are we, oh prophet, to say yes or no,
Ask the people and you'll know.

First elder: We couldn't go now to the people saying:
That's your king; they will laugh at us and stone us!

Samuel: And I thought the people nominated you,
To act on their behalf. Let us all go home in peace.
The proper day will surely come when I will
Show him to the crowds.

(Exit the elders)

Listen, Saul, Go back home,
The donkeys have been found
And your good father is worried about you.

Saul: Back to the ox and plow?

Samuel: What has befallen you? You do not want to? Dissatisfied?

(Looks at him strenuously. Saul avoids Samuel's stare and stammers:)

Saul: I leave…

Samuel: Well, go back to the hills of Benjamin and wait till your time comes.

(Exit Saul)

The son of Kish, how quickly did he change!
With so much sadness, umbrage and complaint
That Saul — had looked at me when saying:
Back to the ox and plow?
Might the peasant challenge
The one who did anoint him?
Calm down Samuel, all the eyes of Israel,
Still look up to Ramah.

(A commotion, people run in)

A commoner: Oh, Prophet, the elders told us that you chose a king!

Samuel: The elders told the truth.

Second: Commoner: Is it also true, his name is Saul?

Samuel: His name is Saul; he's from the town of Giva'a

People: Give us the king, where is he?!

Samuel: Just left the room he's on his way that leads to Giva'a

Voices: He should be fetched!
Run quickly, get him!

(Some of the people run out and bring Saul in)

A voice: He'd better go back to Benjamin!

(Saul is brought back in. He is shocked and afraid to meet Samuel's stare. He is being brought back next to Samuel, and then when he is at Samuel's side and face to face with the crowd, he proudly lifts his head)

Voices: How handsome he is! He's taller than all!

People: Long live! Long live King Saul!

(All of a sudden there's a howling lament coming closer, a man runs in, entirely covered with dust, his clothes torn.)

Messenger: Hear out! Hear out! Listen to me people of Israel!

Voices: Who is crying so?
Who's lamenting so?
What does he want?

Messenger: The murderer Nakhash,* king of Amon,
Attacked the town of Yavesh-Gil'ad!

People: Oh my, what misfortune!

A voice: Say: can't we appease him with some tribute?

---

*Literally: "Snake"

Messenger: Nakhash will sue for peace,
With only this condition:
That every man of Yavesh-Gil'ad
Would poke his right eye!

People: How cruel!
What misfortune!
How shameful!

Messenger: They sent me here, to ask you brothers,
for your help

People: Oy Vey to us!

Messenger: Brothers: please respond!

People: Oy vey to us!

(Saul steps up front)

Saul: Did all of Israel become
A bunch of wailing mothers?
Not your tears your brothers need,
But your blood in battle!
Take a calf and cut it into twelve —
As in Israel is the count of tribes,
And send a part to each of them
And have the messengers announce:
He who doesn't go with Samuel and Saul,
Eschewing brothers' blood and tears,
Will have his cattle fare the same!

Second Act

(After the victory over Amalek, site of Gilgal, warriors and commoners. In the distance one can see the army's tents and cattle and sacks filled with loo. Shofars are blowing)

First soldier: Long live! Long live King Saul!

Soldiers: Long live! Long live King Saul!

People: Long live!

First soldier: See how the nobles praise our king,
It is deplorable and sordid.

First citizen: Didn't we greet you
With bread and water,
Dance and song?

2nd soldier: Not us you are now greeting but our triumph
I recall how yesterday
When walking through the streets
To war against the enemy.
How impertinent you were
And from your open doors and windows,
Mocked us and the king.

Third soldier: The sight of plundered pretty clothes
Draws them out to us,
Noble people, would you want part of the loot?

First citizen: I don't want presents, I'm prepared to buy;
It is conceivable, that you need the cattle,
But the clothes are made of silk and crimson —

First soldier: Do you think that only you,
Cream and nobles of Judea and Ephraim,
The clothing will befit?
It will also fit my wife!

2nd soldier: What are they doing here?
Death to all of them!

Soldiers: Death! Death to all of them!

(The people draw back in fear. The crying becomes louder. Out of a tent come Saul and Avner.)

Soldier: Long live! Long live King Saul!

People: Have mercy, spare us please!

Saul: What is happening? Why the crying?

People: Your soldiers want to kill us!

First soldier: The nobles do deserve to die;
They never wanted you as king.

Saul: Not another word!
The blood of Israel seethes for revenge
Over their enemies, not over the hatred of a king
I want this day to be
Not just a day of setting scores and victory
But a day of charity and pardon!

People: Long live! Long live King Saul!

Avner: You plan to win the people with benevolence?
You're making here an error.
You've lost a chance to rid yourself

Of your greatest enemies;
In your grace they see a weakness.

(They both go into the tent)

First citizen: On the day of our triumph,
We have for you, our warriors, a present:
We have in our cellars, skins of vintage wine.
We told the slaves to bring them here!

2nd soldier: You did not volunteer your blood in battle
So now you'll give the warriors your wine!

First soldier: I'm afraid, that soon we may see
That the wine in the skins is as false
As the blood in their veins!

(A slave brings in a jug of wine, the soldiers drink)

2nd soldier: Oh, this was refreshing!

3rd soldier The wine washed the desert dust
Away from my mouth!

First soldier: (sings)
It is so hard to be a fighter,
But wine makes us much lighter!

2nd soldier: (sings)
It is so hard to get older
But wine makes us younger!

(They drink and sing, their yelling becomes louder, from the tent come out again Saul and Avner)

Avner: The army is now restless
It's hard to curb their reckless senses.

If very soon you won't prepare a feast,
And divvy up the loot —
They could still attack our town,
And rob what Samuel forbade
To take from Amalek, our enemy.

Saul: Don't you know that Samuel forbade
To sacrifice to God without him?

Avner: How long do you intend to wait for him?
The very wind that wafts the smell
Of Samuel's sacrifice to heaven,
Will carry yours as well!

Saul: And who gave me that right?

Avner: The victory!

Saul: What will the people later say?

Avner: You'd like to know that?

(Crying out)

Hear me out, oh, soldiers!
The prophet Samuel was to come
As is the custom: to sacrifice to God.
But there's no sign of his arrival
I know darn well, that you are weary
Of wanderings and battles,
You must be missing, dreaming of your homes.
Where troubled and distress do wait for you
The mothers, wives, and children,
Relatives and neighbors.
And we all want to bring them,
The knowledge of our feats.

Soldier: Avner is right!
Go home soldiers!

Avner: But now, how can we go
And not make offerings to God?
But the prophet strongly banned us
From making sacrifice without him,
And king Saul is very modest
And is awaiting Samuel.

Soldier: Enough waiting!

Avner: Did the king hear?

Saul: Just wait a while… for just a moment…

Avner: My voice is weak… not more than one… Soldiers!
Speak to your king!

(The soldiers circle Saul)

Soldier: King! Bring a sacrifice!

Saul: What do you, Avner, want
To do with me — the king?
You wake in me a passion, of which I'm terrified:
Unbeatable is a woman's lust for her man,
The man — his lust is just muscle and dominion
I go; I try to go up on the stage
But I'm afraid of the occasion when,
I will finally be there!

Avner: Up! Go up! Onto the stage! Go higher!

(Avner helps Saul go up onto the stage. The army is excited, happy shouting. All try to stand as close as they can to the altar. From the road appears Samuel)

First soldier: There he goes!

2nd soldier: There goes Samuel the prophet!

3rd soldier: It's him who didn't want a king!

First soldier: Probably he wanted to anoint one of his sons!

2nd soldier: Why is he coming now?

Samuel: Greetings! Peace upon you!

3rd soldier: Enough! No more!
From today we don't want peace
From today, we just want war!

Samuel: Don't you recognize the prophet Samuel?
Is just one victory from your king enough
So you'd forget your prophet and your God?

(People are stirring; Saul comes down from the stage)

I am already old, my end is near,
So answer now before your God and his anointed:
From whom did I purloin an ox, a donkey — or
Which one of you did I abuse?
From whom did I receive a bribe,
To overlook your sins, speak up!

People: You haven't wronged a soul!

Samuel: And let's today bear witness from them both:
From king and God!

Saul: Prophet, I avow!

Samuel: Oh see! The sky is blue to the horizon
And hanging stiffly over us;
But From the north soon comes a cloud
And just like scouts, right after him —
Glide many other ones, all great and dark.
Oh see: they flow, they merge!
Do you know what time it is?
God is raging! And now in Israel now it's harvest:
In the fields — plentiful is the grain
But God says now: I'm sending hail
It won't be plain, but made of stones.
Upon your gardens, orchards, fields
The rocks and boulders soon will fall,
To bend and break and desolate!

(Hail is heard coming down)

And further God does say:
I'm summoning a thunder!
Upon your homes and stables
And no people and no cattle
Will be spared today!
And over Lebanon,
The proudest cedar be in flames!

(A thunder is heard)

And God is also saying:

People: Have mercy prophet!
Cease your anger!
Do forgive!
Calm your rage!

Samuel: So hear: God commanded me to say:
I See how rife with fear and sorrow —
Your hearts now have become;
So I rescind this punishment
And like before I'll pray to God
On your behalf, and always lead
In righteous ways.

(His voice becoming threatening again)

But if against the heaven and your God you sin —
It will be the end of you and of your king!

(The people and the soldiers step back, only Saul and Samuel remain)

Did you, son of Kish carry the will of God
And wipe off the people of Amalek?

Saul: I have done as you commanded.

Samuel: From where these sheep and cattle
And the sacks of loot in camp?

Saul: The cattle are from Amalek, to sacrifice to God.

Samuel: God has enough of those
That sacrifice the beasts,
He'd rather have the ones,
Who sacrifice themselves!
And who is the Amalekite in camp?

Saul: That is Agag, the Amalekite king.
The people and myself, — we pitied him.

Samuel: Didn't God through me, the prophet,

Command you to desolate and kill
All of the Amalekites?
I know the reason why you spared Agag:
And why you want him near you:
You want him as a standing testament
To your final triumph.
And you let the sheep and cattle live,
To bribe with them the people!

Saul: Injustices that Amalek committed
On our people in the desert
Are long forgotten; victory alone
is much too little for the tired army.
They want the spoils of war!

Samuel: The fruits of victory are not
Donkeys, camels, gold and silver.
The fruit of victory is just — revenge!
And now bring here Agag!

Saul: (calls) Hey, slave! Bring here the king of Amalek!

(Agag is brought in, in shackles)

Samuel: Amalek: prepare yourself.
I am the prophet Samuel.

Agag: (turns to him with flattery)
Till now my ears alone have heard of you
Now I'm happy to behold you with my eyes.

Samuel: You dog, have little reason to be happy!

Agag: I heard that you like justice.

Samuel: Therefore – I shall now dispatch you.

Agag: You want to kill me? Oh prophet,
Have mercy, spare my life!

Samuel: Mercy? That is a word, which had resided on your ears, not on your mouth.
Did you have mercy on the women
Whose bellies you slashed?
Or on the children whose heads
You smashed against the rocks?

Agag: I am still young and want to live!

Samuel: God's world is beautiful and large,
And all the people in it want to live!
You used to think that just to you
The trees must give their fruit
For others there should only be the gallows.
This is your end; the earth
Can't bear you any longer.
From its depths now come the screaming
Of the people that you buried still alive.
The rivers rebel against you:
They seethe with holy blood
Of innocents you spilled.
And willingly the sun would turn its rays
Into a rope for you to hang!

Agag: And I was told you were against
The sacrifice of sheep and cattle.

Samuel: It's true that sheep and cattle cannot pay
For sins of evil men.
For his sins one must pay by himself.

Agag: Must I really pay that much?

Samuel: Our account is old:

When my people ran from Egypt,
You trailed us and attacked us.
And severely punished us just
When we escaped from bondage.

Agag: Give me life and I will fetch you water!

Samuel: Your water, it will taste like bitter herbs.

Agag: I'll cut firewood for you in the forest.

Samuel: That wood, that you will cut for me,
Instead of a bright flame,
Will only give me smoke.

Agag: (Falls at Samuel's feet)
Like a dog at night, I'll guard your house!

Samuel: I will not exchange you with a dog.
At least on his loyalty, I can count!

(To Saul)

Summon here a soldier!

Saul: Soldier! Soldier!

(Enter a soldier)

Samuel: Soldier, lead him out!
(To Saul)
Give me your sword!

(Soldier leads Agag outside. Samuel follows him with the sword in his hand. Saul remains by himself)

Saul: Is that the prophet? I know him not!

In his hand, he held the sword
Like he were no prophet, but a soldier!
I am horrified! He scares me!

(Enter Samuel)

What did the prophet do with Agag?

Samuel: I killed him with the sword.

Saul: (with distress)

And now for my own sins,
will the sword now fall upon my head?

Samuel: I won't raise the sword upon your head,
But it will always be — hanging over it.

Third act

(Giva'a in Saul's house. Mikhal)

Mikhal: (singing)

Don't trust the spear too much my love:
The spear alone will never save you.
For nonetheless — my love is brave,
And renders you in battle grand.

And the battle you'll survive,
My love will be your armor;
Hatred leads you to the war,
And love will lead you back victorious.

Don't trust your arrows much, my love:
By themselves they will not save you,
My love too — is brave and strong,
Defeating hatred far and wide.

From the battle you'll return,
My love will be your armor;
Hatred leads you to the war,
And love will lead you back victorious.

Don't trust too much the sword, my love:
The sword alone will never save you
My love too — is like a hero,
Chasing hatred from the land

From the battle you will rise,
My love will be your armor;
Hatred leads you to the war,
And love will lead you back victorious.

(David is back from battle, Mikhal runs to him)

Mikhal: My David!

David: Mikhal!

Mikhal: Is that really you?

David: It is David, but with a victory richer.

Mikhal: How calmly you now speak,
And I am always filled with fright,
When you go fighting.

David: I was afraid just in one battle,
When your father, promised you to me
If I would kill a hundred philistines.
Afraid that I might lose you.

Mikhal: When you go to battle,
The land is cheerful
But the house without you
Is empty, and mournful.

David: Isn't your father feeling better?

Mikhal: He's getting worse by the day
It seems that whenever you return
With yet another triumph,
His heart should be rejoicing
But he's sadder. It is certain:
He doesn't need your sword
He only needs your music.

David: Even that won't always help.
So I don't see what ails him;

Mikhal: The reason's hard to fathom:
How this misfortune started
I now, can still remember:
As if just now it happened:
The sun was shining bright,
On his throne, was father sitting.
Around him, ministers and servants.
But suddenly — he cried,
Was pale, his head dropped to the side,
His crown fell from his head,
Rolled away to some corner.
We tried to cheer him up, but ever since that time
Peace and cheer have vanished.

David: Didn't the heavens turn cloudy,
And a wild storm start?

Mikhal: Yes. Right. Wait… You know… how did you
Know? Did I tell you that?

David: No, no you didn't…

Mikhal: Did Yonatan tell you?

David: Neither did Yonatan.

Mikhal: So how do you know it, how?

David: That day is etched in my remembrance.

Mikhal: And what happened to you then?

David: On that day of my life, something
Miraculous also happened to me.

Mikhal: Tell me,

David: I cannot say it.

Mikhal: Probably something bad had happened to you:
That's why you want to hide it from your wife.

David: You are mistaken, it was good!

Mikhal: So, you won't disclose what made you happy,
And I the fool, had thought you loved me

David: Oh my Mikhal! When you speak of love
How can I keep from you a secret?
Forgive me! I will tell you all,
But swear to me to keep this secret
From spying ears and strangers.

Mikhal: I swear!

David: At that moment,
The prophet had anointed me,
For king of Israel.

Mikhal: David? Could it be? You — a king?!

David: Why are you pale! You aren't happy?

(Enter first soldier)

First soldier: Oh, minister! Your warriors wish to see you
And wonder where you'd gone. And also
How can we split the loot without you?

(Enter second soldier)

2nd soldier: Oh minister! The prettiest women now
With tambourines are dancing — greeting you,

The bravest minister and your loyal warriors.
You are always the first to go to battle
How can you be the last to get the praise?

David: Excuse me Mikhal, The soldiers are calling.
I am waiting impatiently for the evening
When we'll meet again.

(Exit David)

Mikhal: Oh dear father! Now I've found
The reason for your suffering.
When Samuel anointed David —
That was the time that from your head
The crown had fallen
From your head. Since then —
David had been dreaming of the crown
And father was afraid to lose it.
And I? ... I am David's wife, and Saul's daughter.
I love them both. My heart feels
A great struggle,
Emerging between them.
Do I go with my husband or my father?
My heart is torn asunder!
How strongly I am sorry for my father's pain!
And David how I love him! David!
I'm only a weak woman,
Father do forgive!

(Exit Mikhal. Enter Saul. Dejected)

Saul: In the street — a celebration! And they all cry:
David!
And he, my son, my eldest — with them
They have forgotten me completely.
Enough! Enough! I can no longer hear it!

(closes the window)

Wherever I escape from the crying
It chases after me, it teases me.
My room is a cramped cage.
But the caged bird dreams
Of flying to the street.
And in the street, for me it will be
So much worse!
The sun gets hidden too by clouds,
And must leave the sky at night,
But, how long will last my night?
Who's coming here? It is Avner.

(Enters Avner)

Hello Avner!

Avner: David is already back from battle
And yet again — a winner!

Saul: You too, Avner are taunting me?

Avner: And you, you always send him off to battle!

Saul: I always think that he will lose.

Avner: And now *we're* losing!
Listen to the roaring crowd!
One more victory like this,
And they will make him king!

Saul: A king of Israel, can only be anointed
With the oil of God's own prophet
Not with vile philistine blood,

Avner: The way I hear it, in the prophet's jug
There was some oil left out for David…
Saul: Enough! God has chosen me as king!

Avner: God is always with Samuel,
The king is but a man and can be changed.

(He becomes impatient)

Why beat around the bush?
When I found out, that by war we won't
Be free of him, I had decided To condemn him
As a rebel in a court!

Saul: How will you prove his insurrection?

Avner: I sent a confidant to follow him and listen
And he heard of David saying,
That Samuel had anointed *him* as king!

Saul: How could that be? Oh God! How is it possible?!
Oh, evil Samuel, If God had told you
To anoint another king for Israel —
Why didn't you do it openly
And did it so that all could see?
He went into my house
And wrapped himself around my body
Like a foreign vine around a tree
To rob the sap and leave me withered
For everyone to see.

Avner: I'm waiting for your order!

(Saul looks at him, startled)

I hear you my king!

Saul: I command!... I order… I… (Faints)

Avner: (calls out) Servant!

(Enter servant)

Help the king!

Saul: No, no, I'm better!

Servant: Order me my king. Should I call David?
His playing gives you joy!

Saul: Let it be, you may fetch him

(Exit Servant)

Oh bitter fate!
The source of all my troubles
Will also give me peace.

(Enter David)

David: I am ready, Oh king!

Saul: (To Avner)
Leave both of us alone

(Exit Avner)

David: Should I, king, play the harp?

Saul: Not now, I'd like for you to hear me out

(Saul sits on his throne, David stands before him)

David, you are a man endowed

With great virtues
The very hands that pull the bow with skill
And make the arrows find your foe,
On the harp they pull the strings.
In your hands there's life and death
Life to friends and death to enemies.
And further, still, to get Mikhal
You paid with the life of a hundred philistines.
For love, you'd paid with hatred.
How do you mate — love and hate?

David: I had learnt this once,
When I tended my father's sheep.

Saul: When you tended sheep?
What strength is needed for a shepherd?

David: The shepherd's skill is not to be as weak as sheep
In the meadow, but as strong as the lion and the
Bear that come to chase and steal his flock.
I learned to love the sheep, and the haters of the sheep —
To kill!

Saul: (Looks at him intensely)

And if the shepherd should be weak or ill ?

David: Then he should let another shepherd
Watch his flock.

Saul: (springs up from the throne, upset)

Stop! Enough! The nerve!

(Takes control of himself. Sits again on the throne. After a while,)

People say you write and sing,
Are these love songs?

David: Not love songs.

Saul: Wine drinking songs?

David: No!

Saul: A young man you are,
And you don't want to sing
Of women and wine?
Of what then do you sing?

David: Of heaven.

Saul: I am ready after every battle,
To sacrifice to God some sheep and cattle.
That the smell of my success
Might go in God's nose.
But share my power with the prophets,
That, I never will!

David: How can a man converse with God
And shun his prophets?

Saul: (Suddenly changes his demeanor)

And now say this:
Do you know Samuel the prophet?
Were you once in Ramah?

David: He once came to our town of Beyt–Lekhem.

Saul: Why would he come into your town?

David: To make offerings to God.

Saul: And who did he sacrifice?

David: Excuse me. Who? I do not understand.

Saul: Now hear this: A loyal soldier said to me,
That there's a rumor among the folk,
That the prophet had anointed a new king!
Did you ever hear of that?

David: And did he also tell you,
The name of the anointed?

Saul: (goes close to him and says to him sharply)

The name of the man is: David!

(Through the window can be heard the singing of women)

Saul is in a castle
David in a tower
If Saul is a wind,
David is a storm
Saul strikes a thousand
David — tens of thousands
Praise be to Saul
But to David glory.

Saul: Do you hear the singing of the women?
How nicely they praise and idolize you!
And me, just mention as a favor.
It is certain. Not only, have you won over the
people, but also the bed of the king's daughter.

And from my son, clothes and weapons.
Could it be that soon you'll come and say:
Saul, hand over your crown!
The crown will rest a while longer on my head
And so the spear: and so my spear —
You shall receive!

(He throws the spear at David, David leaps to the side. The spear goes into the wall. David escapes)

Fourth Act

(Giva'a. Saul's house. Saul is alone)

Saul: Traitors! I can no longer trust a soul,
Not even my very own!
Earlier, Doegg the Edomite informed me
(And though a stranger, I do trust him)
That David ran at night to Noob
And the priest there, Akhimelekh
Gave him bread and Goliath's sword.
And another servant also said:
My Yonatan clandestinely sees David.
But when I send my trusted soldiers
To entrap and kill him —
My own Mikhal helps him escape!
Once, I was angrily disfavored by the prophet
For being merciful and graceful to my foe.
If harshness without pity, is a sign of kingly power
And of a king's esteem and wisdom —
Then today I will be so!
Traitors! Your day has come!

(Calls out)

Hey servant!

(Enter Servant)

Was the priest from Noob brought in?

Servant: He is awaiting your command!

Saul: Lead the priest inside!

(Exit servant. Enter Akhimelekh. Falls at Saul's feet.)

Akhimelekh: Oh, my lord, Oh my king!
Your soldiers raided Noob
And cruelly drove here women,
Children sheep and cattle,

Saul: This isn't all. It's only the beginning
Of harsh punishment to traitors!

Akhimelekh: Oh my king I am not guilty!

Saul: Silence, traitor!
I know it all without your Ephod*
Do you deny that in your house in Noob,
You gave bread to David?

Akhimelekh: And if it even were a stranger,
How can one not sate the hunger
Of a man who asks for bread?

Saul: So you claim it was compassion,
Now say this:
Goliath's sword, you also gave to him as aid?

---

* A vest worn by priests used in oracular/prophecy

Akhimelekh: How could I not, give the sword
To the one who valiantly obtained it?
Is the sword not his?

Saul: It's his! It's his!
So he can stab me with it!

Akhimelekh: How could it be? Him? — His Mikhal's father?

Saul: Don't you know that David is my enemy,
That David wants to steal my crown?

Akhimelekh: I'm only busy with the priesthood,
And far and alien are to me the earthly matters…

Saul: Even if the words are true,
It doesn't minimize your guilt;
You know that I appointed you
To counter Samuel, and removed
The prophets from authority.
Against the castle of the prophets at Ramah
I had built Noob, the town of priests.
With your household there you settled,
And there you fattened up.
The first shearing of the sheep you took,
From the orchard, the very first ripe fruit;
And for the smallest sin received an offering
And offering, and offering!
You've made a living out of sins and crimes.
But for your own sins — you must die!

Akhimelekh: The first wool, fruit and offerings, since
Moses' time God had commanded to be mine.

Saul: Only commanded! But never gave!
And remember too, that Samuel taught:

God doesn't seek the sacrifice of sheep and cattle.

Akhimelekh: 'tis true that for your deeds, I'm in your debt.

Saul: Hmm... my debt! You should have paid
A Long, long time ago!
I thought, you would appreciate and aid my rule,
But you surmised that I was weak,
And David's fame is growing with the people;
So you were scared to lose your wealth
And switched to David's camp — you traitor!

Akhimelekh: It's true I gave him bread and sword,
'tis all it takes to punish me severely?

Saul: This isn't all! The priests are singing songs:
For whom their voices soar?
Would it be for the king?

Akhimelekh: The songs are sung for God and heaven.

Saul: And aren't all songs composed by David?

Akhimelekh: It's true that many songs are David's.

Saul: So! You receive from David songs
And pay him back with bread and sword!
Enough! I will no more allow it!
Death to you and all the priests!

Akhimelekh: Calm your rage! I beg your mercy, king!

Saul: Not one more word! Servant!
Execute my sentence!

(Servant leads away the priest. Saul remains alone)

That is the end of all the priests.
No more they'll sing the songs of David.
And not only them:
It shall be known throughout the land:
Whoever dares to sing the songs of David,
Will be like David, held as rebel,
Deserving death from all who find him.

(Pause)

David's songs and prayers are renowned:
Through you the people pray to God.
Crushed in crowdedness and sway in yearning
Against the enemy — with you the army goes
And comes back home always victorious.
With you the shepherd leads his flock
With you the mother lulls her child to sleep
The scythes intone your songs in harvest
On the holidays the girls will dance with you
The river rushes, trees in the forest too.
And I, I'd like to drive them off the land,
But quietly, to myself I also sing these songs…
Oh, I fear your songs more, then your victories in battle!

(A commotion behind the door, Yonatan tears in)

Yonatan: Away Dogs! Let me through!
What's happening father?
Your servants blocked my way
And didn't let me meet with you
I scarcely managed to come in by force!

Saul: Such was my order! What have you to say?

Yonatan: Is it true that earlier you sentenced all the priests to death?

Saul: Are you against it?
I really thought you would be pleased.
You always were their enemy.

Yonatan: Because they stood against the prophets
As you let them take away
The sheep from shepherds
And the fruit from peasants
But this boundless bloody rage,
Who knows where that will end!

Saul: Aha! Now it is all clear and plain to see!
They helped David. And so you too —
The traitors are defending,
First defend yourself, you traitor!

Yonatan: What are you saying father?

Saul: You are defending your friend David!

Yonatan: If you think that with my love for David
I am betraying you, my father,
Then this life you once had given me
As father, you can take away!

Saul: (Softer)
My son, your father will not seek your death
He wants to see you follow him alive.
I saw your blooming, as a miracle,
From child to man, from man to daring hero,
Fair and noble fast and strong.
My father's heart did happily rejoice:
My crown and throne one day will be your own!

Yonatan: I do not know if I'm a hero like you say —
But to you I do admit:
I dream and strive to be a hero!
But to be king, this is for me still far;
A hero — rules his soldiers and himself
In the haste and spurt and heat of battle.
A king — with strict laws and commands.

Saul: Didn't you ever want to rule?

Yonatan: Not to rule with violence
Which subdues the masses
But with the love for individuals.

Saul: And I have always hopped and dreamed
That from my loins will sprout
A multitude of kings and heroes
And make my father's house renowned
For generation, with victories
And wise effect.
I am the first king of my father's house
And do not wish to be the last!

Yonatan: Did the sons of Ali inherit the priesthood?
Samuel's children, did they turn to prophets?

Saul: The children of Samuel and Ali,
Did not reach the stature of their fathers.
But with you — all mothers would be blessed!
I'm really just the son of Kish the peasant,
But you already are the son of Saul the king.
You were reared in the king's court,
Learned wisdom, and the ways of war.
You did not have to learn like me
From errors, trials, blunders, pitfalls;
But right away began with triumphs.

Yonatan: I thank you and obey you, father.

Saul: There are two men in Israel:
Their names are Samuel and David.
I do admit: they're both important.
(And therefore, all the more a danger)
I do not have the strength — to struggle
with them both
But if you'll go with me — I will succeed!

Yonatan: Did any of those two, attempt to steal your throne?

Saul: They rob me of my peace and my esteem!
You do know David's hiding place
So help me get him in my hands;
As long as he's alive, my throne is not secure;
And later you'd be risking the same fate.

Yonatan: I am prepared to serve the king
With sword and spear, but not with treachery!

Saul: (Springs up from his throne)

Is David closer to your heart than is your father?!
How will strangers follow me if my own son
Ignores me?
You are cavorting with my enemies
And won't escape your fate as well!

(Grabs hold of a spear. He wants to throw it. But his hand trembles, and he lets it drop. Yonatan is standing this whole time, and not moving)

Away! Don't show yourself to me again!

(Yonatan leaves, Saul remains seated gloomily on his throne. Pause. Mikhal enters.)

Mikhal: What wants from me my father and my king?

Saul: That he would be your father and your king!

Mikhal: That, he'll always be.

Saul: Don't you bear your guilt?

Mikhal: I haven't hurt a soul.

Saul: And who hid David?
And help him flee from judgment?

Mikhal: David is my husband after all, my husband
and I love him!

Saul: But does he love you? There is some doubt in there,
For he really, also loved Meirav your sister.

Mikhal: And my sister loved him too,
But he is destined just for me
And mine he shall remain!

Saul: Even if he really loves you
You should feel his strangeness
Do you know because of whom?
It is because of me.
You will once lie in his arms
He will kiss you and will hold you
But suddenly you'll see:
His eyes will be extinguished.
His voice will become hoarse
His arm will limply hang around you:
And would you want to know the reason?

(Comes closer to her)

Hear now: a smile upon your face,
Or a movement similar to mine —
Will remind him of me — his enemy.
And he will spurn you and your race.

Mikhal: You only see that which could separate us.

Saul: And what will unite you for long?
If you had with him, a child,
And it happened that your love was lost
You could retrieve your love again
In that child, in that joint soul.
But you're not destined to become a mother.

Mikhal: And God did also close up Rachel's womb
And later gave her, two handsome children
And one was second only to a king!

Saul: You are infatuated with his hero's name
And maybe… later as a king.
Probably you think he'll share the throne with you
But wives of heroes are no heroines
But only one of the hero's trophies
The king's wife is still not a queen
But just one of his subjects;
David's not the kind who shares his rule,
If you want power, pick another man, a weak one.

Mikhal: I do not want another, I want the first,
I'll even be his slave!

Saul: Enough! Do you know Palti son of layish?

Mikhal: And who is he?

Saul: A man who proved his loyalty; I have for long

Wished to reward him.

Mikhal: Father I am puzzled. It is the first time
That you speak to me, your daughter,
Of your people, to be thanked.

Saul: I'm speaking of him now as one
Who will now enter, the circle of my family.

Mikhal: I only love David!

Saul: The child of a king must fill her duty!

Mikhal: (Falls at his feet) Have mercy father!

Saul: If you won't follow the counsel of your father
You'll be forced to follow his command!
Hey slave!

(Enter a maid slave)

Rub my daughter's skin with salves
Dress her up with the prettiest gown,
Make pearls and gold and precious stone
Adorn her head and arms and neck.

(To Mikhal)

As it befits you, King Saul's daughter,
In your full beauty you will show yourself

(Calls)

Amihood!

(Enter servant)

Quickly, saddle up the donkey and call Palti
The son of Layish from Galim.

(Exit servant and maid slave, enter Akhinoam)

Akhinoam: Earlier I met Yonatan, he was so pale,
Not one drop of blood left in his face
I could hardly stop him and
I'd like to know the reason why he is
So sad and bitter, but then he wordlessly ran out.

(Suddenly sees Mikhal)

And why Mikhal is here, and crying?

(Mikhal falls into her mother's arms)

What's happening here? What's happening Mikhal?
Do say!

(Saul is silent. Akhinoam turns to Mikhal)

Akhinoam: The son is silent, the father too,
Both men are stubborn, you speak Mikhal!

Mikhal: (Breaks out crying)

Father wants to separate me from David!

Akhinoam: Is Mikhal telling the truth? Answer!

Saul: I will give you another man —
One much better than David!

Akhinoam: She doesn't need a better man.

Mikhal: (Falling to his feet)

If you'd like it better,
Sacrifice me now to God
Better than to a stranger!

Saul: Samuel and David ought to sacrifice to God
For he does help them,
Smoke from their altar pleases him.
But the one thing that will help me is my strength!

(Exit Saul)

Mikhal: Oh mother! Your daughter did dream that with
Her husband, she would wear the crown of Israel…

Akhinoam: To wear a crown? Do not dream of that my child,
It is better with your man to guard the sheep
It is better with your man to plow the field.
Now look at me: I reign together with the king
And woe is me and wretched I am — your mother.

Fifth Act

(Ramah, In front of Samuel's house. Samuel and David)

David: Oh prophet! I have been running far from Saul.
So many times he'd sent me to the war
To greatest danger, to the front,
And once he threw at me his spear.
He sent his henchmen in the night
To fetch me and dispatch me.
I hardly managed to elude him.

Samuel: Since he vanquished Amalek
He is no more alive,
Just bitter melancholy animates him
And lets him overcome his death.

David: And I? Am I alive? I'm not a king now am I?
If I'm a wind, why did you put me in a bag,
And did not let me stir the sea?
If I'm a flame,
Why didn't you send me to the sea, or
To consume the forest trees?

Samuel: Now David, look at me: once, I was a judge
For all of Israel — now only in Ramah.
I hear of Saul's brute actions
And I can neither help nor save a man
And more than that: even I, am not secure;
His followers could charge Ramah!
I knew it right from the beginning:
That fire which they made me start,
The storm will seize and carry to my house.
Fervent was the will of Israel

And I had thought:
If I must do as they request,
I'll choose for them a humble man.
Obedient, pious and sedate,
I picked up one — and was at fault.
Could it be, that prophets will no longer rule?
But you — why are you so embittered?
You are no prophet but a king!

David: You, a prophet, once anointed me as king,
But didn't give me, the people or the land,
I must win them over — one by one
And conquer every plot.
And no corner of this land is mine.

Samuel: Rest assured; this land and people you shall win.
Saul can barely hold it by aggression;
His children — won't succeed him
And if you'd want to be a king of Israel
And have your power and your house prevail
Always keep it open for the prophets' message.

David: And this is why I have now come to you.

Samuel: But you cannot remain in Ramah
For they know: someone had informed King Saul
That you are hiding here with me.
Twice already, he had sent me envoys
To catch or even possibly – to kill you.

David: Oh prophet, what am I to do?

Samuel: It's clear: you must forsake Ramah today.
Remaining here could bring us grave misfortune.

David: Where to? Should I go to the Philistines?

Hide from the king amongst the enemy?
I'm of this land and love my brothers!
The first words uttered as a child,
The song and laughter of young girls,
In the fields the toiling man –
In the household works his wife,
And the silvery repose of the old.
Or should I to the desert go?
Since childhood I've been bound,
With every hill and valley of our land.
With every stretch of meadow I'm enamored
I'm drawn to all of that and more:
For every sapling is endeared to me
How I can now, still smell their fragrance.
How could I live without it all?

(Enter a messenger)

Messenger: I have been sent here from King Saul
To bring you back, alive or dead!

David: (With despair)
I'm prepared to join you, messenger of Saul.

Messenger: Calm down and rest assured.
I won't deliver to the clutch of death
Our greatest hero; in Ramah I shall remain.

David: Oh, say how fares my wife, Mikhal?
And Yonatan, my loyal friend?

Messenger: The king is sore with Yonatan.

David: Oh, friend! How dearly you are paying for your Friendship. Oh why, messenger haven't you mentioned my Mikhal?

Messenger: In his fury, the king gave her — to another man.

David: Oh, misfortune!
I no longer have a home to come to.
Away! I'll go away from here!
In the desert with the jackals I shall live
In the forest with the wolves to howl,
On the ruins — cry, lament with owls
But go! I will crawl among the rocks
And hide myself of pain and shame!

(Exit David)

Samuel: Great is your despair, but David wasn't born
For gloom and loneliness, but for war, for victory
For glory and for rule!

Exit messenger and Samuel. Enter Saul disguised in different clothes)

Saul: The messengers betrayed me
They all remained in town!
I must capture David in Ramah!
I will not let Ramah as well become
A town of refuge.
I will set the nest on fire,
Before wild birds grow wings and talons
The priests will feel my wrath
And who will dare oppose
When I turn against the prophets?

(Sits on a rock by the house. Pause)

Ah, how many years have passed,
Since I walked upon this place.
I did not have then any kingship
But maybe more, much more: my youth.

It seemed to me back then: once Samson carried
The gates of a city on his shoulders,
For me, that was too little: I thought I could carry
The foundation of the world upon my back!
But it was just a smaller part:
To only carry just the burden of one state,
Made my back hunch over.

(In the distance is heard a flute playing)

I can no longer have my youth.
But who would stop from going back, to be
The humble man that I once was?
But no! He who wore the crown for just a day, or
Even for a moment — will not give it to another.
And if he does, he'd also give his head along with it.

(The sound of the flute becomes closer)

And maybe I should parley with the prophet?
Possibly he's now more lenient.
His sail will lose its restlessness.
And the winds — they would not chase me
Like some dogs in chains.
The shadows will no longer charge me.

(Comes closer to Samuel's house)

Heart of mine stop racing!
When once I came to Samuel's house
A humble man and yet unknown,
I wasn't then that agitated.
Now, I am Saul — a king, a ruler,
So why is now my heart so shaken?

(A group of prophets with harps, flutes, drums and cymbals)

1st prophet: I was walking in the field
To plant it with a seed
Suddenly I heard a voice
Calling me by name:
Listen to the Lord
Be a prophet for Israel!
Herald the truth across the land!
Though danger may be great,
Warn, reprove, demand!
In the field the little seeds
You should no longer plant
Plant the truth within the hearts
Of those who do not understand.

2nd Prophet: I was sitting in the meadow
There the sheep were grazing
Suddenly — I heard a call
That truly was amazing:
Hear the voice of God — now hear
Israel's prophet be!
Herald the truth,
To minister and king
Though the danger may be great,
Warn, reprove, demand!
No more sheep to lead and feed
No more cows and oxen,
Be a shepherd now
For Israel's people!

3rd Prophet I was standing by the clay
Kneading it into a jug
Suddenly I heard
Rushing wings above:
Listen, to the voice of God
Be a prophet for Israel!
Go announce the truth:

To the ministers and king
Though the danger may be great
Warn reprove, demand!
No more clay you'll seek
In the ditches deep
Instead of forming clay
You will now form the people!

1st prophet: What are you seeking, stranger,
By the prophet's house?

Saul: I came here from a distant city.

2nd prophet: What do you seek? Did you lose an object
And want the prophet, to find it?

Saul: The only thing which brought me here
Is fear of losing.

1st prophet: The fear of loss is often worse than
Loss itself.

Saul: Strange but true.
I've heard your singing, and I liked it
Can I also be a prophet? How do you
Conduct your life?

2nd prophet: At times we are impatient.

Saul: How dreadful!

1st prophet: Not so, stranger.
Restlessness drives one to strive and search
And to the highest palace of creation!

Saul: But I'm tormented by my visions!

3rd prophet: Sometimes we too have visions,
But you speak of torments,
What is it that you see?

Saul: I see specters!
And hear some objects tearing.
Threads are flying all around me
Like spider webs they want to trap me!

1st prophet: It is uncanny! Has any one of you,
Oh, prophets seen the likes of that?

Prophets: None!

Saul: I also hear wild sounds.

3rd prophet: Is it the sound of flutes and harps?

Saul: They moan and crow and howl like jackals

First prophet It isn't God that talks to you
But something else,
An evil spirit!

2nd prophet: And who it is that so disturbed your soul?

Saul: A prophet!

(The prophets are taken aback by the unexpected answer)

1st prophet: Who are you to blame a prophet?!

Saul: A king!

(The prophets look at him uneasily)

2nd prophet: Stranger, tell us openly and clearly
What's your name, and who's the prophet?

Saul: The prophet — Samuel! The king is Saul!

(He throws his coat away from him and remains standing in front of them in the attire of the king)

Prophets: It is Saul!
He himself!
What misfortune!

— What does he do here among prophets?
— He will kill us like he killed the priests!

(There is a great panic. From the house comes out Samuel. He looks very sick)

Samuel: What is the noise behind my window?
That took me out of bed —

(He suddenly sees Saul)

Saul!

(He wants to go back into the house)

Saul: (Blocks his way)

You will no more avoid me!

Samuel: (To the prophets)

Prophets! Tell him: long ago I had erased
King Saul from my awareness!

Prophets: The prophet says: I had erased long time ago
King Saul from my awareness!

Saul: Oh prophet, they do know: for you my name is
Still the same as when we met before — Just Saul.

Samuel: Prophets: thus says the prophet:
Saul is dead to him, and I will not
Be here in Ramah to see specters.

Saul: And who called out the specters
Wasn't it the Samuel the prophet? ...

Samuel: I didn't look for his exulted lineage
For me he only was a tool!

Saul: No, no! I will not only be a tool!
I am a man of flesh and seething blood.
The same rain — drops on all the plants.
But each and every plant grows
And blossoms with its own
Fragrance, shape and color.
You wanted me to pledge to your control,
But do you know the worth of such a pledge?
It's only good for doing
As much as I can handle!
If you made a mistake by choosing me,
Then why is a mistake for me forbidden?

Samuel: Prophets! He should know:
I haven't in the least myself forgiven
My own mistake until today!
In my old age,
Ramah has been my castle
And it is, too, my jail.
A sin should never be forgotten!
Justice should be strong as much as evil is:
You were picked by me, to devastate
The enemies of Israel.

You did not fulfill your great assignment
And for me, just like before — you don't exist!

(His voice strengthens)

And in your place, another one shall come —
It's David! Even his greatest sins
That will appear as dark as night,
Will serve so one could see the stars:
Which are indeed his virtues!
It is David! It will be he, who soon
Will free us from the philistines
And from his loins will come
So many heroes ministers and kings!

(His voice weakens, but is still very clear)

And Israel will sing and tell
Of his great deeds, bravery and wonders —
Until the very end of time!

(He collapses into the hands of the prophets)

Prophets: Alas and alack to us! The prophet is dying!
Take him to his room!
Take him to his bed!

(They carry Samuel into the house. it is dark. A storm begins. Some local residents run through.)

First one: They say Saul came to Ramah!

Second: They say the prophet is dead!

Third: Oh, who will protect us from Saul's rage?

Fourth: We will be at the mercy of his hands!

We should run away!
To the mountain!
To the caves!

(They run)

Saul: Stop! Wait a minute… I want to say…
But no one's left… they are all gone…
Why is the street so empty?
Why do they quickly lock the gates and doors?
If they saw a wolf
There wouldn't be such trepidation.
Did I really turn to such a specter,
A horror for them all, for all to fear?
Oh people! The prophet turned you all against me
For I defied him.
How long must I pay for that old sin?
I am now tired… I long for rest… for peace…

Sixth Act

(Giva'a. in Saul's house. Akhinoam. Saul's mother)

Akhinoam: I have been waiting for you very anxiously
And, forgive me for bothering you
It is not only for my sake, but for us both.
Saul's my husband and your son.
What I, his wife, did not succeed in doing,
Maybe you, his mother, could effect.

Mother: What do you want, Akhinoam, tell me clearly

Akhinoam: Saul is in fear of losing his crown,
And I — I am afraid of losing him!

Mother: Is it another woman?

Akhinoam: If another woman came between us,
I would poke out both her eyes.
I would stone her in the street!
But how can I compete with specters?

Mother: My ill son, my Saul! My daughter,
What can I do to help him?

Akhinoam: I want for Saul to leave the city
And go back to his village.
To ease the load of kingship
So he perhaps may find some peace.

Mother: And you'll remain here with the children?

Akhinoam: How could I leave?
We'll both remain with him.
And Yonatan will rule till he recovers.

Mother: Your counsel pleases me Akhinoam.

Akhinoam: You hear? There he goes! He shouldn't know
That we had already met.
I'll wait for you in the room on the left.

(Akhinoam goes down quickly. Enter Saul.)

Saul: Oh dear mother! Oh, beloved mother!

(Hugs her)

Mother: My son, my son! How much you aged!

Saul: Why did you shun my house till now?
On what account my brothers are
Better than I am,
That after father's death
You preferred to stay with them?
So many times I sent messengers
To bring you here into the city
And every time they came back here without you.

Mother: I had thought: I wouldn't know how
To behave in the house of a king.
The high class customs, are so strange.

Saul: But mother, you still came.

Mother: I came here because I heard that you
Are sick and filled with sadness

Saul: It is true. I'm sick, but my enemies

Probably exaggerate it
To hurt my standing with the people.

Mother: My son, what do I care what others say
When your pale emaciated face tells all the tale.
Your brother's beard is black as pitch
(Though he is some years younger)
And yours: how many gray hairs are in yours!

Saul: So what if his head now is dark and mine is white.
He never put the crown upon his head.

Mother: Cursed is the day when you first put
The crown upon your head.
On your head the prophet didn't
Drip some oil but tar. Your brain
Has been aflame since then.

Saul: Oh mother! …

Mother: Quiet! People in the village told me
Of your vile and brutish deeds,
And I was… I was ashamed
To show myself in front of them.
In restless days and wakeful nights
I asked myself: is it really true,
That I had given birth to Saul?
I nursed you from my breast with milk,
Not poison; I taught you to be good
And not ruthless with the weak.

Saul: I wanted to consolidate my realm
Not only for myself, but also for my children.

Mother: For your children? Who would it be then?

Would it be Yonatan who is beloved by all,
But not by you, or Mikhal whom, with
Violence you forced her on another man —

Saul: Who loves her much!

Mother: But her tears soak her pillow every night.

Saul: And I thought that you, mother…

Mother: If you don't want to be a father
Don't ask of me to be your mother!

(Saul grabs his head with his hands. The mother stands next to him. Avner enters. He sees that scene and his face darkens. Saul sits stiffly, but the mother feels the presence of the stranger. She turns to him and withdraws in fear. Avner steps closer to Saul. Finally Saul too, notices him. He is confused and stammers)

Saul: It's a moment of weakness… here, a moment…

Avner: I've come to speak to you of an important matter!

Saul: Why are you standing in the corner? It's not a stranger.
It is one of our own, a relative — Avner…

Avner: (Remains standing stiffly in his prior pose)

I've come to speak to you of an important matter!

Saul: (Sees the mother, who is withdrawn and looking at Avner with fear)
You see: an infrequent visitor — the mother…
Is it possible for you to come a moment later?

Avner: A moment later may bring peril!

Mother: I won't disturb you. I'll go in to see
Akhinoam and the children…

Saul: Forgive me mother. It will be just a moment.
Later I will come to Akhinoam's room to see you

(Saul accompanies his mother out. Comes back and sits on his throne)

I hear you Avner.

Avner: That which I will say, will likely be —
Hard for you to hear.

Saul: A danger that is known is smaller,
Than one that lurks in hiding

Avner: Listen: I know that David is the one
Who brings torment to your heart.
Therefore I circulated in the army,
Not only that he plans
To steal your crown,
But that he also robs the people;
Their wives, their homes, their vineyards and
Donkeys.
(For otherwise your men, wouldn't risk their lives)
David had to run to the desert,
Up the mountains, hide in caves.
And wherever the sun shines,
There he cannot go.

Saul: I know I have a lot to thank you for.
Your loyalty I never doubted.

Avner: But you have doubted *his* disloyalty!
This makes things for you and me much worse!
What I built with toil and suffering

You then destroyed!
David had been chasing restlessly my men
But you, when meeting him,
In front of all your soldiers
Did ask for his forgiveness.
By which you showed to every soldier
That the cause for which he struggles is unjust!
Do you realize, the damage to your reputation?

Saul: Did you really come here to torment me?

Avner: Hear me further:
It wasn't any different with the prophet:
That's the person who rejected you, and still
While you're alive, anointed someone else.
You came to him all by yourself
And asked him to forgive you.
What is the sin that you committed
For which Samuel needs to forgive you?
Isn't it *his* sin that he committed against you?

Saul: I know who Samuel is,
Who David is, and both their sins.
The prophet is from Ephraim, that great tribe,
And David — from the powerful Judea,
Samuel was raised by Ali, and David
Had been blessed by God with virtues.
If both had been supportive of my rule,
Samuel with counsel and David with his deeds,
Then Israel would be great and strong!
But neither one of them had wanted to assist
The simple peasant, run the kingdom.
So the people have remained loyal to me
And they always come
To tell me of David's whereabouts.
He is With Samuel in Ramah
With a small number of prophets;

But indeed the times have changed for
The tables turned around:
It's Samuel — dead, and outside the borders
Of Israel, David soon be found.

Avner: He is outside the borders of Israel —
But he spreads hatred around Israel.
The people see in him a hero, a redeemer!

Saul: And how can we catch him if he hides
Amongst the hated Philistines?
To go against him is the same
As start a war with them.

Avner: Such a war I would avoid.
But now they know: Akhish in Shunam
Had amassed against us a strong army!

Saul: Oh, Dark news! Bad news!
And say yourself:
Is it now the time to speak of David,
When every moment the enemy's
Army is preparing to attack?

Avner: You will not prevail against the Philistines
Their might is just too great.
They have chariots and weapons.
They may be bribed away with gold
And maybe too, some villages and towns.

Saul: No, no! I will not let it happen!

Avner: You would be able that to say
If in your hands you had the weapons.

Saul: And what will say the people of Israel?

It will be a disgrace for generations!

Avner: To distract the people from our impending loss
We'll present them with a second enemy,
And over him we shall prevail!
The enemy, ought to be none but David.

Saul: And how will you catch David?

Avner: If to the Philistines we give some bribe
And furthermore, some villages and towns
We can make this one condition:
That they should extradite the rebel David!

Saul: Your advice thought up the devil!
I will conduct a war against the Philistines!

Avner: You can be calm – for your opponent is David.
He had you in his hands so many times
And did not hurt you; but he is still your foe;
My enemy is Yoav,
From him I can expect no mercy!

(Enter Yonatan)

Saul: Let Yonatan…

Avner: I know his answer in advance.
He will not stand against David.

Yonatan: What does Avner want here?

Saul: Avner earlier relayed
That Akhish had amassed
The philistines in Shunam,
For a war against us.

Yonatan: This day we should prepare
Our force against them!

Avner: It is useless! Our army is too small
And also lightly armed!

Yonatan: Should we give ourselves to slaughter like
A herd of sheep? No Avner, No!

Avner: And if we lose the battle?

Yonatan: No one ever loses a war, in the cause of freedom!
Every battle for justice is a winner!
And even if the enemy sometimes wins
Hate against the enemy grows up seven fold
Until the men light-up with new resolve
And win, and must prevail.
Here I go with you and our brothers.
And Avner, you as well: you who once
With me did fight so many battles
In which your part wasn't too small.
This war is our duty! It is holy!
We lack weapons? Let no one fear.
With sword with lance,
With sticks and stones!
Not only we defend our land,
But also save our honor!

(In the background appear Saul's mother and Akhinoam. They are engaged in conversation)

Akhinoam: While Saul needs rest… and peace…

Saul: (Stands up, off his throne)

Let Avner order all the messengers to come.

They should blow the shofar across the land
In the name of God, In King Saul's name —
Wake up Israel! Prepare for war!

(Akhinoam Falls powerlessly, But Saul's mother supports her.
Two soldiers come and blow the Shofar)

Seventh Act

(In Ein-Dor. A military march sounding weaker and weaker.
In the house of the Sorceress.

Tirtsa: It is the first time that in our little place
One, for once can see so many soldiers.
No one's left in their own house,
From young to old — all are outside.
I came out in front of the army, for I
Wanted very much to see the king.
So many years tormented by the enemy
And had no chance to see his face.
They say, he's hounded by bad spirits.
And more: that he really came here
Earlier, in disguise.

Aviyah: And I saw there, mother, you know who?
The king's own son, the youngest:
Malkishooah!
He seems to be my age
I never saw such a handsome boy!

Tirtsa: It's not for you to dream, my daughter,
Of a prince. Only in stories and in songs
It's told of meetings with
Plain girls such as yourself.

But today, you should very much beware;
The city's filled with men of war.
You are still young, and not inured
And they — their battle day awaits tomorrow, and
Makes today their actions rash! Go to sleep my
child!

Aviyah: If I could only sleep today!

Tirtsa: My daughter: only bats and owls
Fly at night with open eyes.
People at night — should have them closed.

Aviyah: So why you too, can't sleep at night
Why do you walk around awake?

Tirtsa: Older people cannot sleep,
Because old people in their dreams
See their youth and have remorse;
The young— they see the future in their dreams
And wake up happy right at dawn.

Aviyah: What of my prospects do I know?
But you, of your rich life, how many wondrous
things you told me of! And not the least —
Of days gone by.
Even now when down the street
We walked along —
No, not at me they look, men look at you…
I am embarrassed, but today I have to say:
I am still really young, no more than fifteen years
And — forgive my impoliteness, mother…

Tirtsa: Forgive me daughter, in my life,
My beauty always was a curse!
I was still young, much younger than you're now,

That men, have always looked at me as I
Was walking in the street
And if I looked at one,
He would turn pale, his senses thrown into
Confusion. I would give him a light smile,
He'd blush. Samuel knew the wondrous
Power of my stare, and called me to
Remain in Ramah, and said:
You shall be like Debora the prophet!

Aviyah: What are you saying? You, a prophet?

Tirtsa: I stayed among the prophets,
And learned to play the harp
Back then the prophets sang too much
And so they didn't pray enough
But then I was unwell. Their songs
Were silenced; and stronger, hotter
Were their prayers.
Samuel lost his power over them.
He summoned me to him and said:
Go right away from here!
Your power's not from God but
From the devil!

Aviyah: And so, you left because of the prophet's anger?

Tirtsa: I was away, but not alone
Many others went with me.
All becoming sorcerers
But my stature much exalted than was theirs
From all of Israel came to me the crowds.
From the very start, people seek
What is unknown and not allowed.

Aviyah: And you really used to heal them?

Tirtsa: I really healed only the people who
Believed that I could help them.

Aviyah: What did the Prophet Samuel do?

Tirtsa: Fearfully he watched my magical city
Which cast a shadow on his prophets' castle,
And he was powerless and lost
Until he did anoint Saul for a king.

Aviyah: But Samuel was upset with Saul!

Tirtsa: Later… later, when he found
That Saul, just like myself – will become
Stronger than him.
When the king was on the throne
Samuel gave him a command
To eliminate sorcerers from the land.

Aviah: And how did you survive?

Tirtsa: Saul's servant came one night to kill me

(Silence)

Aviyah: Go on, tell me more!

Tirtsa: He was slender, young and gorgeous
And it was a red hot night

(She keeps her silence, as if she wants to think up something; finally she speaks)

Hear me out; I'll share with you a secret
That I kept from you till now.

Your father did not fall in battle
When I was pregnant with you
(Like I told you all your life).
On that summer night, he gave us both,
The gift of life…

Aviyah: Tell me quicker, tell me more,
Is my father still, somewhere alive?

Tirtsa: Early morning when I left him
He was lying in calm sleep
When I ran away here to Ein-Dor.

Aviyah: And him? What happen to him? Say!

Tirtsa: That night he came to Giva'a,
And Saul ordered him brought in
And hung from a tree as punishment.

(Knocking on the door)

Someone knocking on the door! A visitor, that late?!
Could be someone from Saul's army
It's better he won't see you here.

(Leads her daughter out and comes right back,
Again, knocking on the door)

Tirtsa: Who's knocking? Who's knocking that late?

A voice: (From outside)

A Soldier!

(The sorceress opens the door Saul enters, disguised)

Tirtsa: How dare you soldier, disturb a woman's sleep
That late at night?!

Saul: Now calm down, woman. I am a soldier
One of Saul's, and I came here to conduct battle
But not with you.

Tirtsa: And what do you seek soldier?

Saul: People of Ein-Dor had told me: in your cellar
There's some old wine, and since I too, am old,
Let's have old wine restore an old man's youth!

Tirtsa: Sir, the wine is kept in the cellar for guests
And great celebrations,
And you are to me an entire stranger!

Saul: (Throws to her a purse with money)

The Shekels are no strangers!

Tirtsa: (Takes the money)

Allow me sir, the wine to bring you from the cellar.

(Exit Tirtsa)

Saul: Secretly from the tent I stole away
Under this mantel, hiding in dark shadows.
Once when I had such a heavy heart,
David used to play his harp,
But now, it's wine which will inebriate
And hearten me!

(Enters the sorceress)

Tirtsa: Sir, try a drop of this upon your mouth, and

You'll agree that it paid to wait for it that long.

Saul: (Drinks)
The man who in the cellar hid the wine,
Turned weak and old, sick and gray.
He died, and his body — all destroyed.
But the wine had bubbled, and from year to year
increased in strength.
Now, many years after its youth,
It is — still exuding might!
Oh woman, isn't this in equal measures,
Full of wonder and of woe?

Tirtsa: You are still sad because you are still sober.
But think, how this wine, that you imbibe
For all these years, did keep its strength
To make you happier.

Saul: (Offers her a cup)
You are a smart woman, here, drink! And be merry
as well!

Tirtsa: (Drinks)

Such a long time since I drank wine.
Do tell me, soldier, who you are.

Saul: And why would you want to know?

Tirtsa: Because your visage, voice and movements
Testify of great torment, and equally of great rule!
Other than Samuel's face, I haven't seen all of my
life,
A face as such as yours.

Saul: And in your face, there lies enchantment!

(Sorceress trembles)

If I were only bolder, healthier, younger —
But only ashes now remain of me.

Tirtsa: Try to kindle the ashes from below,
They probably are smoldering with fire!

Saul: More than your wine, your words, they made me
Drunk! But no more drinking — Farewell woman!

Tirtsa: What scares you soldier?

Saul: Death is no shame for a soldier,
But he should be ashamed, if captured and turned prisoner!

Tirtsa: How would you know, who captured whom?
Stay here with me! Stay here till dawn.

Saul: How can I be with you serenely,
When my tomorrow is unknown and dark
And my heart is filled with restlessness and worry?

Tirtsa: Would you like to see your future morning?
I will now tell you a great secret,
For which I could pay with my life,
If it's revealed to Saul the king.
(Though a woman could sacrifice her life for whom she truly loves)
But I would do it even though this may become
My final night, I will show you your tomorrow
Through my magic.

Saul: And where did you learn your magic?

Tirtsa: The same one who taught the birds to sing,
The people to breath, the stars to shine,
The rivers to flow, and the wine to intoxicate!

Saul: That one, turned away from me
And did not accept my best offerings.
So let it be through magic — that I find out!

Tirtsa: To God's prophets come the angels,
Down from heaven, and to them
Reveal the future.
But to me the ones who speak are ghosts
The ghost of which person shall I summon?

Saul: Call out the ghost of Samuel, the prophet.

Tirtsa: Oh, no! Anyone except the prophet!

Saul: Why not him? Was he your enemy?

Tirtsa: There was a time when he came close to me,
But later he pushed me away.

Saul: I too, had suffered the same fate,
But you promised: are you having second thoughts?

Tirtsa: Only for a moment, a moment's hesitation,
Which I'm already overcoming.
I'm ready to summon the ghost of the prophet!

(It is now dark. Lightning and thunder, storm.
Enter the ghost of Samuel)

Samuel: Who summoned me hither?

Saul: (Saul falls on the ground shaking)

Saul!

Tirtsa: (Screaming)

Saul?

Samuel: You disturbed my peace when I was among the living.
Give me peace when I am in my grave!

Saul: I was punished by your rage,
You became my fear and horror
From which I could not separate
Until it so depressed me
But also elevated me
And with your death I lost my last support.
Even as an enemy, you nonetheless, gave me strength.
Therefore, I am coming to you again,
Looking for counsel and salvation
Here you can really see yourself: even death
Cannot pull us apart.
I received from you my kingship
And with you it could be ending.

Samuel: And what is your desire, what would you like to know?

Saul: At dawn I go against the philistines
I want to know if I shall win
Or God will turn his people into the hands of
Our hated foe — to rob and murder and enslave us.

Samuel: No, not through you, God will fight the philistines
For that he's chosen David.
And you — you will lose the war.
And in the war will perish with your sons!

(Saul falls powerless on the ground. Samuel's ghost disappears. The sorceress comes closer to Saul)

Tirtsa: It is really Saul! Him, the same Saul
Who made each moment of mine fearful
And through the nights, for years,
Robbed me of my sleep!
Because of him I was buried like a mole
Kept away from people and the sun,
He sent his men to search for me,
And follow me like dogs
If not for him what would I lack?
I would be dressed in silk and clover
With gold and silver — all adorned.
I would have been renowned in Israel
And Egypt.
I carried this in my own heart
With hatred and with fear for many years —

(Pulls out a knife)

I was always ready, to plunge the knife into my heart.
If caught by one of his assassins,
But now —

(She readies to pounce on Saul with the knife. Holding it high for some time. Her hand begins to shake. She lowers it.)

What are you doing, have you lost your mind?
On whom are you raising your hand?

(Throws away the knife, attempts to revive him)

Wake up my lord… my king… my love…

Saul: (Wakes up)

Is he no longer here? Did he disappear?

Tirtsa: What did the prophet say?

Saul: Defeat and death — together with my sons!

Tirtsa: My love, now that I found you,
Must I also lose you — the same night?
No, no! You will prevail against your haters
Tomorrow it will be a wondrous shiny day,
I will meet you when you're back,
And with me all the women
Playing harp and flutes,
With drums and cymbals and with dancing —

Saul: And that which the prophet earlier told me?

Tirtsa: Do you really believe in witchcraft?

Saul: By witchcraft you summoned Samuel
But when Samuel showed himself to me,
You lost control over him and he told the truth.

(He takes her by the hand and leads her to the window)

The same moon in the heavens
Will shine again above,
But my face will be paler.
And my eyes, though they be open
Will not see anything but starring cataracts.
My head will be severed by my enemies
And hanging from the city gates,
To horrify our people with my death
And no one will be seen around,
But around me — the crows be flying, crowing!

Tirtsa: And if you really do believe,
That you will lose the battle
And tomorrow you must fall,
Why show up for a guaranteed defeat?

(Comes closer to him and whispers)

You must decline to fight tomorrow!
And if it doesn't fit you to withdraw,
Let Avner lead the war.
Here I will prepare for you a bed,
And bring you food.
I will serve you tenderly,
Like no other woman could.

(She notices his reluctance)

You really are not well, you have a fever!

Saul: Do you think that a king of Israel
Will run away from battle
And hide in bed, or in the arms of a weak woman?
I will lose — that certainly could happen
A hero doesn't always win,
The main thing is — not to lose one's freedom
And to resist until the end!
My army's waiting anxiously at camp.
The Shofars ready, to blow up a storm!
I must go away before the stars fade out.
I thank you woman for your warmth!

Eight Act

(Gilboa'a mountains. The Israeli camp. In front of Saul's tent. Saul)

Saul: I saw David earlier, in a dream.
Sneaking slowly through my camp
Until he came up to my tent.
I yelled and called, for the guards!

And still, when I tore out of sleep
His voice was ringing in my ear
How calm and quiet all around!
The fields wait for the dew
And I have, a premonition that
Soon at dawn they will be soaked
In human blood.
In tender nests the birds are sleeping
And in their dreams they're flying, flying…
Hearing unfamiliar tunes,
But they know and feel that soon
The arrows bringing death will fly
They will hear the screaming, groaning,
Wheezing,
Of the wounded, soldiers dying.
Now my soldiers are still sleeping
Some — in the shade of a ficus tree
Some in a woman's arms
But soon, they'll be awakened
By the sound of the shofar,
Barely knowing that, the enemy
From their night will rob— the warmth of women
And from their day — the shade of trees
Out to battle! People of Israel, to battle!

(Enter Avner)

What good news do you bring, Avner?

Avner: I walked through the entire camp
Ensuring guards are tending to their duties

Saul: And the spies we sent to find about
The enemy's numbers and their arms
Did they return?

Avner: They all came back from their surveillance
And say as one: the enemy's numbers
Are like grains of sand
At the seashore.
And they also say:
In the Philistine encampment,
Are David and his men.

Saul: What would this news mean, Avner?

Avner: That very simply means:
With his hatred he stands against
The people of Israel and their king.

Saul: (Covers his face with his hands)

Oh David, David: in my heart
I always had great fear of you,
But I never hated you.
But now — my heart is filled with hatred!
If I could only send it as an arrow
Straight to your betraying heart!

Avner: Command the soldiers to prepare for battle!

Saul: Order to blow the shofar! Storm the enemy!

(Exit Avner)

Saul: Oh, God of Israel! My soldiers put their lives
Into my hands, do not punish them for my own sins!
But if you want to punish me —
Wait till I come home from battle
And by Giv'aa's gate, strike me with a thunder,
So that I don't profit from the glory of my winning!
But now — help, and give a victory to the people!

(Enter a messenger)

Messenger: I come from David…

Saul: Death to the traitor!

Messenger: Oh, lord Oh king! Calm your rage, have mercy!

Saul: Didn't David join the enemy?

Messenger: David wanted to fight alongside with them
But the enemy did not consent.

Saul: Does this diminish the betrayal of the traitor?!

Messenger: My lord called me into his tent
And told me to relay as follows:
— Go to Saul the king and tell him,
That with the Philistines is David now,
So in the battle he will strike them from behind
And help your army so.

Saul: So, does it mean that David meant to help me?

Messenger: He'd wanted, but their leaders
Wouldn't trust him. They didn't let
Him stand with them in battle.

Saul: For this news, oh messenger — be blessed!
Do not be happy do not triumph, enemy,
Israel has no defectors!

Messenger: Allow me sir to return to David,

Saul: You can return to him in peace
And when you're there, do say
You met the king in his own tent
Prepared for battle with his foes
And not just him, but his sons too
As it befits the loyal sons of Israel —
To fight beside their father!

(Pause)

And also say to David, messenger:
If God withholds from me his favor
And I fall on mount Gilboa'a,
I ask David, when he's crowned as king
That for the sins of father,
He shouldn't punish his descendants…
And not erase remembrance of their names…

(Hides his face and cries. The messenger leaves. Pause. The blowing of shofars is being heard. Clamor of war. Enter Avner)

Avner: The soldiers are fighting like lions
Penetrating through the enemy's first line
And then the second and the third;
With their teeth and nails they

Tore the iron armor of the philistines
But bravery alone is not enough.
God will help the left hand,
But the right hand,
Must be guarded by a sword.

Saul: This army fights heroically,
But we, their leaders are to blame
We didn't give them any weapons!
Therefore: let us fall together!

Avner: I do not want to die! Order the army
To end the battle, to surrender!

(Enter Yonatan, Avinadav, Malkishooah, soldiers)

Yonatan: Out of camp we went, and into battle
The enemy beat us into seven fractions,
Everybody ran out greatly terrified.

Avner: No more victory for us,
The only way to our survival is — escape.
We have to do this soon, before
We are surrounded.

Yonatan: No, no escaping! Only about face
And gather in another place.

Avner: It is pointless fighting to the end!
The leaders of the people should not be abandoned,
In future calamity and pain — Israel will need us
Yet again!

Saul: I will never run from battle!

Avner: Let's try to save some of your sons —

Yonatan: Here I stay

Avner: Perhaps Avinadav, or Malkishooah?

Both: We stay on the battlefield with father!

Saul: I thank you! Now tell the warriors:
If someone wants to spare his budding life,
His sheep his cattle, children and his wife,
If someone's heart is weak and fearful,
He is now free and let him save his life!
And you, Avner, will be with them,
So that Israel may still have a minister

Avner: I will strengthen Israel in its day of pain
And prepare the people for
Avenging what may come today!

(Exit Avner. Remain only Saul, his three sons, Saul's arms bearer and soldiers)

Yonatan: Stay here father with your armor bearer
With your sons and with the rest of your combatants.
They will defend the mountain from the enemy.

(Exit all except Saul and his armor bearer The racket of war becomes ever closer)

Saul: The sun is glowing in the middle of the sky
But a chill goes through my body
For if an arrow hits any of my sons,
It just the same will pierce my heart!
Go up upon the rock, my armor bearer
And tell me how the battle is progressing.

(His armor bearer climbs on a rock)

Armor bearer: The philistines are coming closer.
They're crawling on their hands and knees.
Here a philistine just raised his head
Oh, good he just received an arrow
From Avinadav
Right in his forehead

Saul: Blessed be your hand, Avinadav!

Armor bearer: Swiftly three of them are rising,
One received an arrow in his chest
The second one struck in his leg,
The third pulls out a sword
Oh no, he pounces on Avinadav!

Saul: Oh, God, protect my son, my Avinadav!

Armor bearer: He has no arrows left!
But without fear with his bare hands
He pounces on the philistine
And tries to wrestle the sword out of his hand.
The Philistines is fighting, clings with hands and feet — Oh, alas!

Saul: Say, what happened there? Answer!

Armor bearer: They both fell in the chasm!

Saul: My son, my dear Avinadav!

(hides his face in his coat and cries)

Armor bearer: A wagon just showed up a philistine in it
In colored cape, with armor and a sword —
A great champion he must be for sure!
And even possibly it's king Akhish!

Saul: (Jumps up)

If it's Akhish I will challenge him myself!

Armor bearer: Malkishooah is hasting to confront him!
He wields his sword, left and right
Cutting a path, he's reached the wagon,
The philistine is sharply turning now
His horse to Malkishooah,
Oh, Malkishooah, stabs the horse in his stomach
The horse falls on him — Malkishooah!...
But here jumps Yonatan!

Saul: I cannot bear it!
I can no longer sit that far away!
No, No! I will not die upon these rocks
In grief and idleness.
I too, will fall in battle by the sword or arrow
You, philistines, do tremble
Here comes the conqueror of Amalek!

(He jumps down from the rocks; his assistant follows him running and yells:)

Armor bearer: My lord, my king!

(Enter Yonatan fencing with several philistines)

Yonatan: Shame on you, four against one?

Let one of you — the boldest,
Spar with me!

Philistine: And you will fight against him,
Like your hero David — with sticks and stones!

Yonatan: It is surely a great honor
For you to fall by sword,
A honor I should pay you!

(Fences with them. One falls, then a second. but when he wrestles with the third, the fourth one stabs him from behind)

Yonatan: Stabbed me in the back, shame on you coward!

(Enter Saul with bloody sword)

Saul: Where are you Yonatan? I saw you earlier
Surrounded by a throng of philistines —

(Sees two philistines and Yonatan lying wounded on the ground)

Oh, Dogs!

Saul: (Fences with philistines, stabs one then the other)

Yonatan: Oh Father, you came?

Saul: (Kneels next to him.)

What is it Yonatan? Are you wounded?

Yonatan: I am dying…

Saul: You cannot die before your father!
Live Yonatan! You must live on!

Yonatan: I saw you in your life oh father, often hounded
By bad spirits,
But now, today I see you calm and great,
A king, a hero, you're my father! …

(Dies)

Saul: Oh God, Again he saw me as the king,
And at the same time I am no longer a father
In one hour I have lost my sons!

(The racket of war is becoming louder and closer. Enter his armor bearer.)

Armor bearer: The philistines are very close to us!

Saul: I do not want to be caught alive!
For them to rejoice, and mock me.
If only I could be their prisoner like Samson,
And take with me to death so many of my enemies…
But what's the worth of such a triumph
When you're blind?
Unsheathe your sword my helper,
And quickly stab me in my heart!

Armor bearer: My greatest duty, I was taught was
To carry into battle, the king's armor,
And protect him from all danger.
But no! It will not be,
That the one who must protect you,
Will raise his sword, to kill you!

Saul: There are times when staying alive,
Is worse than dying.
Of that danger now it is your duty
To protect your king!

Armor bearer: How could I raise my hand against
The anointed king of Israel?
How will I show myself outdoors?!
They will point at me a finger:
Look, look! There goes the king's assassin!
How shall I answer to your mother,
When she recognizes me among the thousands,
Pounces at me and yells:
Oh people, he's the one who killed my son!
Free me of this order. I'd rather you command
That I should stab myself!

Saul: Oh, earth, do you recognize me?
It's really me, it's Saul, the son of Kish
The peasant of Benjamin
Recall: still in my youth I tied with you a bond
To give to you my sweat.
Samuel took me far away from you
And I pledged that if an enemy
Would set his foot upon you —
He shall pay you with his blood!
Now his blood is flowing,
And I declare: through sweat and blood and tears,
You will again belong to our people!

(Pulls out his sword.)

Oh Mountain of Gilboa'a, do bear witness for us all.
Tell the coming generations, how
For the freedom of your nation — fell KingSaul,

The first king of the people of Israel!

(Falls on his sword, and after him, his armor bearer, does the same)

END

King David

A dramatic poem

Originally published in Yiddish by
the Federation of the countrymen of
Galitsia in Buenos Aires, 1956.

Characters:

David	The King
Yoav	David's chief of the army
Akhitofel	David's advisor
Mikhal	
Bat-Sheva	David's wives
Ma'akha	
Amnon	
Avshalon	David's Children
Tamar	
Shlomo	
Uriah	Bat-Sheva's first husband
Avner	Late leader of Saul's army
Ishboshet	Saul's son, inheritor of his throne
Rekhav &	
Ba'anah	Officers from ishboshet's army
Avishag	David's maid
Amasah	Avshalom's chief of the army
Khushay Ha'arky	David's friend
Yonadav	Amnon's Friend
Elazar	Ishboshet's court minister

David's wives, Elders, people, messengers from the philistines, Etc.

Act I

First scene

(In Hebron, in David's palace, David sits on his throne. By his side: Yoav and Akhitofel)

David: Yoav, you have often counseled me
Judiciously and wisely,
Akhitofel, you have done the same,
And even though you have reported
This particular affair
I shall not keep among us any secrets,
And hear you both as one.

Yoav: Be it as it may, I have no wish
To keep my sword concealed,
And keep in mind, my king, that Avner
Has against you crowned Ishboshet.

David: Is he not a son of Saul – the King?

Yoav: And 'cause he is the son of Saul the king,
He merits our foremost hatred;
It has often come to pass
That Avner's men invade our borders
And also slay the guards.

David: Maybe Avner told Ishboshet the reverse;
That *we* invade *their* borders. So forget this
Talk about the people of Israel shedding blood!

Yoav: And it will be this blood that's shed
Until you have the little quarrel at the end
Transform into a larger war.

David: And what would be *your* counsel Akhitofel?

Akhitofel: That Yoav is mistaken, soldiers think that victory
Can always be attained by sword.

No bloodshed! The blood that's shed can stain us
And king David for all time.
I have a different kind of weapon:
We should bribe Avner's men and then
They shall be brought into division
And destruction. Showing one side
The weakness of the other, and all of them the
Weakness of their king Ishboshet.

David: I have considered both your counsels
I believe that both will serve to fortify
The house of David, for days and years to come.
But why hasn't either one of you bespoke of
Vital triumphs that we had in recent times?
Who were we? – Traitors, rebels.
Dispersed upon the desert sands,
Each one of us to our shame, like animals in hiding
And with no justice too, and even dying,
But now, now see how it all came to order:
It is to me that Judah's handed – to a king;
It is Yoav, who is no longer leader of a gang of thieves,
But is the king's own minister of war.
And Akhitofel, is a master counselor to the king.
Each passing day our stature grows
Each and every day our camp is growing larger
And all of Israel – we shall win over.
But know you how? Not by waging war
Against Avner, but against the Philistines.
The people will find out who helps protect them
And each victorious battle against the Philistines
Will also bring us victory for our people.
Herewith – an end to the dispute!

(He stands up from his throne)

I thank you both for faithful care of your people and your king.

(Yoav and Akhitofel leave, a slave walks in)

Slave: Army chief Avner, would like an audience

David: I am waiting for him.

(Slave leaves, David addresses Akhitofel)

Leave me.

(Akhitofel hides behind a curtain, Avner comes in, David rises from the throne, gets in front of him, embraces him and gives him a kiss)

Avner: *(Touched)*
Ah, King!

David: Just like in olden times… call me David.

Avner: I haven't earned that much favor.

David: When in my hand I held the shepherd's staff,
It was your sword that executed wonders.

Avner: And yet I have become your adversary.

David: I know Ishboshet was the shadow
On which your image threw a crown;
But people say that you have had it,
Playing 'round with shadows.

Avner: Yes, I've had enough, and come
To beg you to forgive my sin.

David: My clemency can wash your yesterdays,
But what do you resolve of doing now?

Avner: From today, I have decided, to pledge to you my service. Through many years, my name has brought terror to our Foes, and respect In Israel. I bring with me a lot of Battle know-how and experience, and with it, just as certain:

All the tribes of Israel.

David: I am ready with delight to grant you your request.
With Yoav you will conduct my army.

Avner: To victory and fame for our people!

David: Only one condition I have for you: the wrong that Saul
Against me had committed, you should right.

Avner: Which means, my king?

David: You should return to me my wife, my Mikhal.

Avner: I'm certain that your wife you shall receive.
Now, I will go to see the elders
And to them I'll say: it's David's time.
For Saul's survival I had led the battle,
And David, long ago became the same, since he as well
Is now a king.

David: Go in peace!

(Avner leaves)

With the people, Avner's name is held in high esteem:
To me he will bring all the tribes;
And also it is good that Yoav will receive
One more commander for the army.
He serves me faithfully but he was wild and cruel.
He often casts on me his frightful mien.

(Pause)

Why did I order to bring back Mikhal? Do I
Still love her? I dread the moment of the meeting
Though it's good to know I'll have Saul's army chief
And daughter. only one remains, Ishboshet.
But I will not take steps; he will fall, out of his own

Confusion and incompetence.
(David leaves, enter Akhitofel)

Akhitofel: We have succeeded! No longer is Yoav the leader of
David's entire army, now both of them must struggle
With each other and the winner will be the third –
Akhitofel!

(Enter Yoav)

Yoav: You are still at the king's side Akhitofel?

Akhitofel: King David held me over for a counsel.

Yoav: Less advice and more weapons and good battle!

Akhitofel: The hedgehog has strong armor,
A man has but his skin to serve as his protection.
And yet the hedgehog fears the man and man —
Doesn't fear a hedgehog.

Yoav: I dislike metaphors!

Akhitofel: It's forever been the temperament of fools,
Of that which they don't comprehend, to say:
That – I dislike.

Yoav: Impertinent dog!
For such words I would have let you taste the edge of
My sword, but it is only used to drinking the blood of the
Bright battle field of war and not to be smeared with the
Feces of the cripple, the hunchbacks and deformed.

Akhitofel: I know that the leader of an army is one that can
Immediately see the people:
The strength, the form – the whole essence,
But not the slaughterhouse determines the output of
The war, but the preparations.
Your struggle is by now the twilight of the war, and so

You think that you will gain all the fame from a
Victory in battle.

Yoav: By your own words, come out that Akhitofel, that in his
Hand no sword yet ever held,
That he, the coward, perforce leads all my battles,
Ha-ha, ha-ha, I see you now in armor,
With sword and spear drawing arrows from a bow, at the
Head of the army, riding a white horse, what a scene, what
A joy to behold!

Akhitofel: Who knows when *I* will stand heading the army,
A second one, however, will soon be here.

Yoav: It is a lie and it is nonsense! None exists.
There is no second to Yoav in Judea.

Akhitofel: None exist in Judah, though it may be in Benjamin.

Yoav: How could an enemy lead David's army?
Have you lost your mind?

Akhitofel: Sometimes it happens, that a foe becomes a friend

Yoav: Only when he lies dead at my feet.

Akhitofel: He will not lie dead at your feet. But like you, will
Stand at the head of an army.

Yoav: Enough with riddles! Say his name!

Akhitofel: It is Avner

(Enter David)

Yoav: Is it true my king, that it was Avner?

David: It's true.

Yoav: And you didn't slay the dog?

David: Yoav, you have forgotten where we are:
You still think we're in the desert
Or somewhere in a den of beasts.
It had been handled there quite differently
It was needed to take action swiftly.
But now you are in our capital city of Hebron
And you are the army chief.
You must rein your savagery.
I need your sword; not for Israel,
But for the Philistines, Amon and for Moav.
There is a law in Israel,
And the keeper of the law – is the king!

Yoav: Yes, you are a king, and so is Yoav, Yoav
And no other – is the army chief.

(Exit Yoav)

Akhitofel: How dare he be so rebellious?
I'd have him cut off from the army!

David: Your judgment is too hasty.
A man as brave as Yoav
Is very hard to find.

Akhitofel: I believe that there's another.
Do you also just as Yoav,
Think that he, who leads the army in a war,
Must be tall and strong?
Didn't you still as child, defeat
That hero Goliath?

David: It happened so with one – Goliath, and with one – David.
But try and place yourself at the scene of such a battle:
The Philistine camp – strong men,
With bows and arrows, spears and swords

And against them – Judah's army:
Small children, in their hands just slings and stones.

Akhitofel: I stand by my opinion: in everything just as in war
The most important thing is – the leader's wisdom!

David: It seems to me you'd want me to hear
That you too, like Yoav, could be an army chief.
And Yoav thinks that besides being head of the army
He could also be my counsel.
It would be woe to me and Israel,
When one would do another's work,
Now, old friend, come, let us go for a stroll,
In the garden the olive trees are already blooming.

(Both exit. Enter Yoav)

Yoav: The king imagines that in Hebron, in a city,
The wolf would readily become a dog.
It will be Yoav who will not
Let fate be settled by the hand of others.
I have learned where Avner is, and
Sent for messengers to call him hither.
I thought that after my reluctance,
David would have given him another answer —
So now *I* will!
(Avner comes in)

Avner: Hello Yoav.

Yoav: Avner, I've heard that you saw the king,
And offered him your service.

Avner: Yes it's true.
I wish to give him my people and my army.

Yoav: And who is it in your army that survives?
Only hunchbacks, lame and crippled.
And what weapons have your soldiers?

No spears, no swords, no bows and arrows.
But clubs and stones and ancient horns
To terrify the enemy – with blowing wind

Avner: Ah, so much impudence and mocking in your voice.
When first I came to Saul, there was no army whatsoever
I've taken people from behind the ploughs,
And they learned to string a bow and hold a sword.
From farmers and herders Avner built
Israel's first army!

Yoav: And with that army didn't win a single battle,
But David and myself continuously gave chase;
Nor a hero was King Saul:
Seeing that he was losing the battle
And could fall in the enemy's hands –
He threw himself upon his sword.
He did a death of honor choose,
And so his chief of army has already chosen,
The disgrace – of saving his own life.

Avner: To go on living after such defeat,
And raise again the house of Saul
Is of necessity more strength and courage
Than desperately thrash about your sword.

Yoav: You still do praise yourself, with your repulsive acts
And indeed, since you resolved to cling to the
House of Saul until the end –
You've earned your pay from David's sword.
But David's full of mercy and compassion –
So turn back to your family and home,
If you have any strength remaining –
Put yourself behind the plough or else
rock your grandchildren to sleep.

Avner: There is no force that will prevent me from service
To my people, till my final breath!

Yoav: That, you have accomplished: until your final breath.
After your last one you don't have to!

(Plunges his sword into him)

Avner: What power in that hand of yours
How strong and deep you drove it!

(Avner falls down, David's ministers, soldiers and people run in)

Voice: What's happening?
Who cried?

(They see Avner lying on the ground)

Avner!

Avner: It is Yoav, who killed me from behind,
I'm dying… how hard it is to die like this…
It is fitting for a warrior to die in battle
By the hand of Philistines, not by a son of Israel…
And maybe I deserve the punishment
I was ready to betray the house of Saul…
Forgive me Saul, for this capital sin
I'm dying… how hard it is to die like this…

(Dies)

Second scene

(In Mahanayim, at the house of Ishboshet)

Ishboshet: I thought I would be sleeping peacefully.
But sleep, it seems, comes only
To those who are in peace.
How did I embark upon this road? How is it possible?
For fear of losing the kingdom,

I acted hastily.
Which puts me, in greater danger still!
I've held a lofty view of men,
Which gave me such esteem!
But how could I permit Avner approach
Ritspah, my father's mistress,
Was it not a silent hint, that he was ready
To usurp my throne?

(Pause)

Two years in Israel I now have been a king,
And not achieved the smallest thing without Avner.
But I alone became a king.

(He cries)

You hear? – Me alone, alone now king!

(Makes a menacing pause)

You soon will taste the magnitude of my resolve!
At my feet will lay Judah
And David too will serve me as a slave
And I will be a king — over all of Israel!

(Pause)

And Avner's not in sight, Avner isn't here.
Perhaps he did already come, I'll ask.

(Cries)

Elazar!

(Elazar enters)

Say: wasn't Avner here?

Elazar: No my king.

Ishboshet: Wasn't here, and perhaps you might have heard –
Where he is now?

Elazar: In Hebron,
He wishes from now on, to serve King David.

Ishboshet: He just as well may serve the Devil!

(Elazar exits)

Ah God, Avner has indeed abandoned me!
He will no more come back to me!

(Hides his face in his hands. A pause. Uncovers his face – all at once)

It isn't proper that a king should whine,
A king must be proud and commanding
I should punish this traitor harshly and severely!

(Calls)

Elazar!

Elazar: Oh My! Terrible news –

Ishboshet: I will hear nothing now, but issue a command!
Now hear: It should be told in all the towns
That Avner has become a traitor,
And whoever catches him should kill him!

Elazar: This is done.

Ishboshet: What is done? Speak clearly!

Elazar: They say that Avner is already dead.

Ishboshet: Dead? And who rendered him dead without my orders?!

Elazar: They say it was Yoav.

Ishboshet: Yoav?!

(His face covered with horror)

Then Yoav can still come to me!

(Steps back)

If Avner is already dead, I should have someone else
To take his place.
One couldn't find among my ministers a man
More brave and loyal than Zabadin.
Elazar! Call hither to the king – Zabadin!

Elazar: They say he has joined David.

Ishboshet: The traitor! Get me the minister Yoezer!

Elazar: They say he ran away to the mountains or the desert
Hiding from Yoav.

Ishboshet: He left me too! Is there any of my ministers remaining in the house?

Elazar: There's no one left.

Ishboshet: You are lying!

(Grabs him by his throat)

Elazar: Have… have mercy my king!

Ishboshet: *(Lets him go, calms down)*

Eh, forgive Elazar,
This is because of anger against the traitors.

You can already go.

(Elazar wants to go)

Elazar! Wait a minute.
I… command that the guard should
increase around my house!

Elazar: There is no guard,
They've all escaped in terror.

Ishboshet: Cowards! A curse upon their heads.
But still it's good that you remain loyal to me.
Elazar my dear, don sword and shield
And stand by my door to guard
The peace and safety of your king.

Elazar: Do forgive my king… I have a wife and children
And from my elders a nice estate…

Ishboshet: *(Pounces on him)*

False dog!

(Elazar runs away)

Is there really no one remaining loyal to me?
Not a minister, not a servant, none of the guards?
Have I really become abandoned, such that
Any moment can someone from the street
Come and rob me, or god forbid –
What do I hear? – Steps! People go there. To run?
Ah God, run where? Hide where?
It is too late by now!

(Enter Rekhav and Ba'anah)

Who are you?

(Rekhav and Ba'anah are silent.

Say: what do you want?

Rekhav: We have come here for we've heard
That Avner's dead.

Ba'anah: That Avner can no longer punish us.

Rekhav: We have rebelled against Avner
And regret our deed.
We now want to offer you our honest service.

Ishboshet: *(Pleased)*

Aha, you have regrets… seems certainly,
That your sins I should forgive –
A moment… I'd like to think…

(He presently walks away)

A great wonder!
The disloyal have become good friends
And haters – want to serve with honesty
And loyalty.

(Turns around back to them)

I have deliberated and decided:
I am forgiving you your sins.

Rekhav & Ba'anah : Thank you king!

Ishboshet: And for your love, because you've shown me loyalty
When all my friends abandoned me –
I will elevate you:

(To Rekhav)

I nominate, you in Avner's place: chief of the army!

(To Ba'anah)

And I nominate you to be the king's secretary!

Rekhav & Ba'anah: Hurray! Long live the king!

Ishboshet: I will announce in Israel this morning,
And now – I, in the house alone remain
This nation is restless. Yoav's minions spread
Among the people panic rumors.
So set yourself up by my door
And guard so that my peace is not disturbed.
Today I ruled alone in Israel!
Alone have I dismissed old ministers,
Alone appointed new ones in their place
I have accomplished much! Now I am tired
And I'm hot.

(Yawns)

Now, I will go to sleep.

(Goes out in the background)

Ba'anah: How quick it came about! Congratulate me,
For I've become the king's right hand!

Rekhav: And I am the king's chief of the army.
I doubt however, that I should rejoice.

Ba'anah: What are you saying? Have you ever in your life
Dreamed to see such an event?

Rekhav: I feel anxious; we haven't chanced upon
Any of his ministers, have they all abandoned him?
Are we the only two who are loyal to this man?

If Yoav finds out – he'll cast his fury on both
Of us – along with Ishboshet.

Ba'anah: It is true.
We must therefore be quickly gone from here –
Or we may, god forbid, be late.

Rekhav: I dread to think that we are late.
Because who knows how many people Yoav
Has, who watch who comes to see the king.

Ba'anah: *(with dread)*

We are already lost for sure!

Rekhav: And yet a last resort presents itself.

Ba'anah: What last resort?

Rekhav: Kill the king.

Ba'anah: What are you saying?!

Rekhav: If we kill the king,
Then our course here is no crime but mission
That will be rewarded.

Ba'anah: This is just too horrible!

Rekhav: It is still better than be killed instead.
If Yoav's not afraid of anyone
And Avner, that great minister he killed,
Then what are we to him?

Ba'anah: This is all correct,
But I could still not kill the king!

Rekhav: Then hear me out: our people are divided
Between Israel and Judah. A conflict,

Continuously aflame between them both.
And it sheds our blood on both sides.
Will there ever be peace?
There is however good advice:
Out should go one of the kings!
And who do you suppose,
David, or Ishboshet?
Would it be David, that wise and heroic man,
Or there, that one — the fool and coward.

Ba'anah: You are equally saying that you'd want him dead
For the sake of the people.

Rekhav: I also have this purpose.
It is good indeed this coming together
Of both purposes in Israel.
Whether he's a murderer or a hero
Killing a King is a hard thing to do
Whether he later would be cursed or
Indeed praised by his people.

Ba'anah: Were he only a farmer or a shepherd,
And not anointed by God!

Rekhav: You are mistaken:
Not God – he was only anointed by Avner!!

Ba'anah: Were it only evening. In the dark, it would be
Easier for us to kill him.
In midday a murder becomes gruesome!

Rekhav: And maybe I should for you eclipse the sun?
Put an end to it, I've had enough with your disputes,
We should quickly put ourselves to work!

*(Ba'anah goes in the back, Rekhav drags on for a while
Longer. Ishboshet hears steps and gets of the bed)*

Ishboshet: What's going on?

Rekhav: You are in danger!

Ishboshet: From whom?

Rekhav: From… from us!

Ishboshet: What are you saying, people?
You have firmly told me that
You will serve me faithfully.

Rekhav: The weaker should but serve, and not be served.

Ishboshet: What is it that you'll do with me?

Rekhav: Kill you.

Ishboshet: *(cries)* Murder! Help! Help!

Rekhav: *(Draws out his sword from its sheath)*

Will you be quiet?!

Ishboshet: *(Falls down to his knees)*

Remove the sword! I fear it, it is naked!
I'm telling you, I swear to you, no more crying!

Rekhav: Get up!

(Ishboshet gets up)

Why did you become king?!

Ishboshet: Ah, Minister! I have never even wanted to become a king.

Rekhav: But you did!

Ishboshet: Only when my father fell in battle
Had Avner me commanded, to become a king.

I feared to disobey him
For he was strong and harsh.

Rekhav: Just the same, you should regardless, die.

Ishboshet: But not at present! I still want to live!
Indeed until tomorrow, and still, after tomorrow! ...

Rekhav: A day more or a day less – It's just the same!

Ishboshet: *(Falls down to his knees again)*

No! No! I fear death! I tremble to
Even look at the sight of a corpse!
I, also, therefore, never went to battle.
Not during my father's life, not even when I –
After I became the king of Israel.

Ba'anah: And you have never seen a corpse?

Ishboshet: Dear me! I have seen my slain father!
The Philistines, severed his head to show it
To their people, and nailed his corpse to
The wall. I went to see my father's body.
Hanging from the wall, naked with no head
And bloodied.
The cranes flying above him.
Landing and tearing up his flesh. I
Still shudder when I think of it.
I beg you; pledge to me, not to remove my head!

Ba'anah: We are not cruel!

Rekhav: *(To Ishboshet),* he is right,
Here you have it in the ribs.

(Stabs him)

Ishboshet: Oh, my! *(Falls dead)*

Rekhav: *(To Ba'anah)* just one prick and I'm already done!

Ba'anah: *(Trembles all over)* Oh, come away from there!

Rekhav: Wait a minute.
How would you now, have David see
That indeed we have dispatched him?

Ba'anah: My head is not capable of thinking.

Rekhav: If your head cannot think of an advice
And neither can mine – then, his head will help!

Ba'anah: *(Wondering)*
What do you mean?

Rekhav: That it's better for us both
To bring his head to David as evidence…

(He bends down over Ishboshet's body in order to severe the head. Ba'anah is standing and looking at him, startled)

Act II

First scene

(In Hebron at David's house, David is bewailing Avner's death. He is standing and speaking to his people)

David: Though without a crown, Avner was crowned by two kings of Israel.
My heart is filled with woe, as if I lost, not a warrior but
A war and even though he was felled by an assassin,
Bury him, as if he died in battle.
He died for his people and his king!

(The people leave. David remains alone, despondent, Mikhal comes in)

Ah, Mikhal!

Mikhal: David!

(They hug and kiss. After a little while they separate)

Have I changed?

David: You are… You became more womanly.

Mikhal: You might even say, older.

David: And I?

Mikhal: You have become manlier, stronger;
It's harder to keep track of those qualities in you.
Have you been thinking of my hard fate?

David: I've thought so many times about your suffering,
In the arms of poverty, in… a stranger's arms?

Mikhal: Was this from pity or from love?

David: *(Answers quickly without reflecting)*

From love! But why not also form pity?
Didn't your man cause you suffering?

Mikhal: Oh, no, he was very kind.
I felt very guilty.
Why couldn't I for his great love,
Indeed reply with a little friendliness.

David: And how have you lived there through the
years?

Mikhal: In the beginning when I came to him,
I locked myself up in a room
And neither he nor others were admitted.

A servant used to hand me through the window,
A jug of water and some fruit.
That was enough to keep me.
And he would stand there fearfully,
Calling, crying begging me, but I wouldn't
Even grace him with a word.
I'd always waited for some news from you.
I had believed that you would come
And forcefully release me from that house.
But you did not...

David: Do understand Mikhal...

Mikhal: And I always waited for you, hoping...
Hoping even, when they said
That you've already taken...
A second wife.

David: I was lonely, Akhinoam showed me
So much love...

Mikhal: And also when you took the second wife,
I still, stubbornly, did not relent,
But when one day in battle,
Fell my father, Yonatan and two more brothers –
It then became so hard for me to bear
In solitude all the great pain and sadness
And I gave in, and I broke down –
The door opened but you should know:
He used to hear from me "my dear" but never
Heard "My love"

(A slave walks in)

Slave: Two strangers here to see you

David: Tell them to come in!

(Slave leaves; enter Rekhav and Ba'anah with a sack)

Rekhav &
Ba'anah: Hail the king, long live the king!

David: Who are you?

Rekhav &
Ba'anah: Officers from Ishboshet's army.

David: What do you want?

Rekhav: See you free of all your enemies.

David: And what have you done to convert your
good will into deeds?

Rekhav: We have already executed our deed.

David: What kind of deed is that?

Rekhav: It lies inside the sack.

David: What kind of a deed is it, with which
You are ashamed and need to bring me
Hidden in a sack?

Rekhav: A great deed it is:
There lies the head of the king's greatest enemy!

David: I love to take the heads of my enemies
Not from a sack but in the battlefield
With sword,
And now — show me the head!

(Rekhav and Ba'anah take Ishboshet's head out of the sack, Mikhal, who during the conversation was standing in the corner, came near them, soon she lets out a mournful cry)

Mikhal: Ishboshet, brother!

David: Why did you kill the king? Answer!

Rekhav: We have removed your last obstacle of becoming
King of all of Israel.

David: Yes, it is therefore befitting that you be rewarded.

(He calls)

Guards!

(Guards step in; David points at Rekhav and Ba'anah)

Get the two murderers out of here and execute them!

Guard: You have ordered my king!

Ba'anah: Oh My king, have mercy!

David: Guards, Take them away!

Rekhav: You will just the same, not escape your death
So, die like a warrior not a coward.

Ba'anah: Why should I be punished harshly?
I didn't even touch him.

Rekhav: *(in wild anger)*
A lie! I stabbed him in the breast
And he stabbed him in the back!

David: Lead out the assassins!

(The guards lead out Rekhav, others take out the struggling Ba'anah. David bends over Mikhal who is lying on the ground crying)

Calm down Mikhal…

Mikhal: My brother, my brother!

David: Did you hear my sentence of the Assassins?

Michal: I heard…

(Suddenly springs to her feet)

I am left all alone, all alone!
I have just lost all that was mine:
My father, Avner and my brothers,
Only you, you alone remain for me.
You protect, comfort and love me…

Akhitofel: The elders of Israel are waiting, my king.

David: What do they want?

Akhitofel: They want to submit to you.

David: Ah, long awaited day, you came!

Akhitofel: I can already see them,
Anoint your head with oil
And how you will carry the crown of all of Israel!

Mikhal: Forgive me David… I cannot now rejoice, it is
A second head I see before me, that of my brother
Without a crown and it drips blood, not oil.

David: Now I will walk you to your room
You are still tired from your journey here,
And are distraught because of the events,
The dark events. All you should have now is repose.

(To Akhitofel)

Start with the elders in my name, I
Won't be long. I shall quickly come again.

(David leaves with Mikhal)

Akhitofel: David's luck is great: others do for him
His work. Avner was slaughtered by Yoav and
Ishboshet — by two murderers;
I am all for this, that you should be the king
But I resent that in addition you remain
Righteous and clean, know how to wash your hands
And calmly say:
You see, not I have spilt the blood…

(He goes out and comes back with the elders)

You'll have to wait another moment.
I think that waiting is for you a virtue
For— if it were not,
You wouldn't have waited for so long
To resolve to come to David…

(The elders stare at one another)

Yes, not too much value for the mission,
Avner is dead, and also is Ishboshet,
Whom can you now uphold?
And who can stand up to David?

(Comes close to them and looks at each one)

What I want to know is really something else:
Tell me, who were you in the past?

First elder: I was elected by my tribe, after the previous elder –
A friend of Saul had been removed.

Akhitofel: *(To a second elder)* and you?

Second Elder: I've been an elder for Saul's house, but to David,
Always loyal in my heart…

Akhitofel: In your heart? Only in your heart?
It is too little!
You cannot now, just with remorse, escape your sins;
You need to act:
As soon as you have heard from someone in your tribe
A word of discontent and mutinous affinity,
You must immediately acquaint *me* with the matter.
Not David, who does struggle with his foreign enemies –
But me.

Third Elder: Do you mean that we the elders, should amongst our people
Be his spies?

(Enters David)

Elders: *(Bow)* Hail The king!

David: Peace upon you, elders!

First elder: Since the time of Joshua there hasn't been an equal
To you and to your bravery in Israel!

David: *(To third elder)*

You, older Zachariah, years ago I used to meet
You in the house of Saul: I will hear you – speak!

Third Elder: Hear me out my king,
And you, my young friends in years and
In opinion. Yes! I am one of those elders
That Israel sent to Samuel the prophet, for a king.
The prophet for his part forewarned us,
But when we did not yield,
He, at the end had to give in.
And though King Saul had suffered a defeat
In battle with the Philistines, I am still— just as before
In favor of a ruler and a king.
Israel should have a king.
One that is skilled in waging war,

That can protect against the evil enemies.
And since no such a man in Israel exists,
A man who could, like you, so much accomplish,
I will therefore, to you, now pledge my tribe.

David: I take your tribe into my government, and will
Protect it like my own Judea.

Third Elder: Allow me too, to pose a question:
In Israel you have tormented many people
With the Philistines you were once allied.
And your friend once was Akhish, the King.
Therefore the rumors spread that with Akhish
You cut a deal, his yoke you bear and he
Would pay the rent.

Second Elder: How dare he speak thus to our king?!

Akhitofel: Allow me king…

David: Be silent, Zachariah is correct.
I won't allow that the suspicions
Will flourish under cover.
To king Akhish I went not out of choice
But when I had to flee.
And never for a moment did forget
That I was in a land of enemies,
That have forbidden us to carry sword and bow –
So Israel may only be a nation of women.
I won't forget the people's shame!
And never forget mine.
I ran away to be in Gat, escaped the force of Saul,
I was identified and marked for death —
Therefore I had to make believe I was insane:
Singing, dancing, grimacing;
Writing on the walls, and drooling on my beard
And children pelted me with stones,
I swear I'll get revenge
For your mean shame, and mine.

Elders: May forever live David our king!

David: *(To Akhitofel)*
Order the shofar blown,
And ready a meal: bread and wine and fruit
And a lot of meat from sheep and cow and
Make the celebration last three days and nights!

(Mikhal comes in)

Mikhal: From the window, I looked out to the street
And saw the elders leaving,
And among them Zachariah
Was it truly him? Or were my eyes
Deceiving me? – I must now find out!

(She runs out and soon encounters Zachariah)

Ah, good old Zachariah, how happy,
How glad I am to see you once again!
I have lost everyone…

Third Elder: You have found David again.

Michal: I do not know at present, Zachariah.
You were the closest to my father, and knew me as a little girl.
I wish that you stay here at court, and that we
May always remember those times.

Third Elder: Time has flown away my daughter,
Many sins has David carried out, and
In the future probably commit some more.
None of which will be so grave, that for a victory
The people won't forgive, and David hasn't lost
A battle yet.
I am a well that has run dry and should be sealed.
It should not scare a person with its emptiness and
With its dumbness.
I must now live with just the memories:

In them, Saul is a king, you – a princess,
But you are still young, learn to forget…

Second scene

(In David's house. The wives, David)

Wives: From the battle comes the king
To his people what he brings?

Abigail: From the enemy's land he brought
Entire herds of cows and goats.
And bows and arrows, spears and swords
Armor made of copper and gold.

Wives: From the battle comes the king
To his wives, what did he bring?

Abigail: From the enemy's land he brought,
Many dresses, fabric, cloth,
Pendants, rings and colored sash
Ointments and perfumes to splash

Wives: From the battle comes the king,
For himself what did he bring?

Abigail: He did bring a young slave girl
And wants for her a palace built
To her he is already a slave
A bad master for his wives.
It is this way, the king will lead; to him
We must always be true,
It even gets us pretty jewels
The king however, he brings arms.

Akhinoam: *(to Abigail)*

King David loves to hear songs
You should sing to him.

Abigail: I am willing to teach you this song so
That you can sing it to the king.

(The wives laugh)

Akhinoam: And now Avital, it is your turn.
A little less brainy song from Avital,
But with more fire!

Avital: I have a song. I heard it from a girl in my village,

Wives: Sing we'd like to hear it!

Avital: Deep in the forest in the grass,
A secret fountainhead there hides.
No one it did refresh or kiss,
This spring.

Walks a young man on the road
He is thirsty and forlorn,
The spring of water there he sees
And falls beside it on his knees.

As the young man had bound
With the fountainhead, he found
His fervent lips the spring had grasped
And stirred them up.

The young man had fast disappeared
And the spring quickly forgot
But a whole sea couldn't blot
What the young man lips provoked.

*(Egla, one of David's wives, begins to dance,
The others clap their hands. Mikhal walks in)*

Mikhal: Is this the King's palace or a tavern?

(Egla stops dancing at once)

Avital: Why did Egla stop dancing?

Eglah: You see, however, of all things, Mikhal…

Avital: Then is that Mikhal?

Mikhal: Do you want to turn the king's house into a tavern?

Avital: And who are you to dare insult the king's wives?

Mikhal: The first wife of King David – Mikhal.

Akhinoam: This happened years ago, when David wasn't
yet a king.
Of the king's wives, I was the first!

Mikhal: Two first wives together isn't possible
A man can only love but one at a time.

Avital: David can love four wives at once.

Mikhal: Oh god what words!

Akhinoam: And whose son will later be a king?
Could it be yours? – No! it will be mine,
My Amnon!

Hagit: And are you possibly as pretty as Hagit?!

Abigail: And possibly as smart as Abigail?!

Avital: And possibly as slim as Avital?!

Eglah: And possibly as young as Eglah?!

Michal: And yet, what did you get for all your virtues?

Akhinoam: The king had given me a string of pearls!

Abigail: And me, a necklace!

Avital: Me – a dress, of silk!

Eglah: And me a new harp!

Ma'akha: And to me, he brought perfumes!

Mikhal: Maybe once you sought his love,
But now you have enough – presents.
So you secretly look from the court,
for more…

Avital: You certainly miss the stuff, since you are
Too old to get more…

Mikhal: Shameless!

Avital: Old donkey!

(Avital pounces on Michal and pulls her hair)

Wives: So, so! Give to the privileged!

Eglah: The king is coming!

Wives: *(With terror)* the king is coming, the king!

(They scatter, only Mikhal remains. David enters)

David: What's that noise? Who cried?

(Sees Michal) What are you doing here Mikhal, so disheveled?

Mikhal: These wives of yours…

David: Enough with the wives!
You tell me, then, of what should David think:
Of the wars with the Philistines
Or indeed of how his wives behave?

Mikhal: And I totally believed, that you'll protect me from this lot
And strictly let them know that Mikhal is the king's first wife,
So that I can bear it all.

David: Forgive me Mikhal…
(He comes closer to her)
Mikhal…

(He kisses her)

Mikhal: *(Falls in David' arms and breaks out with a cry)*

David!

David: Calm down.

(Mikhal cries stronger)

Enough, enough crying!

Mikhal: So many times I wanted to be with you
And every time there was another wall;
It was Yoav by your side or, Akhitofel.
Haven't you ever been drawn to my side?
So bonded and so filled with memories
Of young years and first love…

David: That's why I did not seek you:
I began my life near you — as boy
And must now, but live with our past.
The king of Israel is forbidden, to

Surrender to a moment's weakness

Mikhal: Where are you David, younger David?
I see your harp for weeks already standing
In the corner shamed, forgotten, its
Strings are mute.
And since I came to you in here,
I have seen once: in haste you threw together
Some jagged, crooked lines.
But they weakly lay and begged, lamenting:
Conclude it master, we want to be a song!

David: There was a time when I still sang,
But there comes a time when one is sung about.

Mikhal: Ah, how you've become so filled with pride!

David: I did not get the crown from my own father.
Since I was a boy, I've been immersed in battle.
First against Goliath, and later with your father.
So many battles!
And later, hiding in the caves and wandering through
Deserts, mountains, in hunger and thirst and fear of wild beasts,
And of informers of your father Saul —
After many perils from these animals and half a life
On a tough road, I transformed, from a shepherd to a king.

Mikhal: Yes you've risen – became grand,
And I went down. I have already lost
My father, mother, and my brothers.
And you grew and expanded, with wives, with
Concubines and children.
Of all the people close to me, there lives but one
But he – he lives but not for me.

David: What do you want?
The shadows of the dead may obscure
The smiles of children;

It sometimes comes to pass with trees in spring:
There: see already all its branches green,
And from the branches singing praise to life
Open multitudes of buds
But behold: it is misfortune, amid the branches
One is dry embarrassed by the spring.
What do you think? Should indeed all buds
Because of that, close up?

Mikhal: How harshly you now speak!
Can it really be, that I've become
A shameful withered branch?
From whence have you that gathered,
From where?
That comes from long loneliness and sadness
And yearning for you. For years I've seen you
In my dreams and thoughts. Had I forgotten your
Eyes – by night from heaven I would have picked
The most beautiful stars and said:
These are David's eyes.

David: You have frozen me too long in your reminiscence.
You talk to me as if you have forgotten,
That I already have,
Many wives and concubines.

Mikhal: That shows that you are still in course of searching;
That you still haven't found the one, and you
Should have a one, just one that you will truly love.
Barely once encountered, your long suppressed emotions
Will swiftly burst and rupture, and
Will not stop or stand, not even for a sin or crime!

(Enter Yoav)

Yoav: Emissaries have come here from Aram,
They carry breastplates full of gold and copper,
They are waiting, to bestow them upon you, my king.

David: I'm coming.

Mikhal: What are the breastplates good for?
Throw away your rigid breastplates,
Gold and silver, copper, iron –
I wish you showed yourself to me now
Without a breastplate –
So I can hear, your human heartbeat –

*(Grabs David by the arm. David tears himself away
And runs out. She pursues him. When she is by the door
She suddenly sees Yoav, who is standing at the opening
Dressed in armor, holding a spear and blocking the way.
He stands cold and dark. She trembles with horror
and slowly, slowly falls away with a cry)*

David! David!

Third scene

(Nigh time. At the foot of mount Zion, three soldiers conversing.)

First: Again and again the Jebusites had repelled our army
From their fortress!

Second: Not just repelled,
Probably a half of us are lying there with deadly wounds –
At the bottom of the fort…

First: You want to joke, when our army is
Fighting so heroically and boldly.

Third: The fortress of Zion is surrounded on three sides
With deep and narrow valleys and it is protected from
Without with steep rock. It's hard indeed, so hard to scale.

Second: The rocks haven't suddenly sprung,

The valleys weren't dug last night.
David should have seen this from the start –
Without letting us spill our blood.

Third: King David! King David is coming!
Back; run back to the tents!

(Everybody runs out, Enter David and Akhitofel)

Akhitofel: I feel how day by day the army's
Discontent increases.
This army has engaged in a heroic battle
When they saw their enemies by the gate
But haven't lived to overcome and capture it.

David: These people often see the danger, only
When it is at hand. But a wise king should
Foresee it and avoid it.
Men should know, must know –
How to defend themselves
But wait with patience till the
Enemy reaches our gate, our barn,
This happens often: not defensive, but too late.

Akhitofel: The kingdom of Israel is still young.
It didn't have a chance yet to emerge
Out of a state of war.
If we lost the war, we first will lose
Respect from all the nations and then
Also that of Israel
It's not allowed for us to stop!

David: Our land is surrounded by enemies
How can I conduct a war with all these
Outside enemies while in the middle of this land
Sit all our tribes apart from one another.
What separates us then from Jerusalem?
Which is the border? It is here, as there,

The same earth, the same heaven
And in the heaven – the same God
That once to Abraham asserted, that this will
Be our land – all of it!

(Enter a soldier)

Soldier: Three emissaries from the Philistines are awaiting you

David: They should be given food and drink immediately
And later, a bed to rest
Bring them here to me at dawn.

Soldier: They are impatient; they ask to talk with you
At once.

David: They may come!

(Soldier leaves, emissaries enter)

First Emissary: We have been sent here from Akhish our king.
The king, and blesser of our God Dagon.
He ordered us to tell you this:
He once heard that your tribe of Judah
Had selected you as king
And he has quietly approved that choice.
And later when you were anointed
As a king of *all* of Israel – he was silent.
He considered you his quiet loyal servant.
And what belongs to a servant
Belongs perforce to his master, but you
Show disobedience. Your effrontery and pride
Increased and you forgot where you must
stop.

David: What is king Akhish saying to me?

Second Emissary: The great king Akhish has ordered, through
His emissaries to tell you this: you are raiding
The fortress of Zion, and would expel the
Jebusites from there.
That means that Israel for you is not enough,
That you also wish to dominate some foreign nations.
This is too much! Enough! You must now immediately
Withdraw from the fortress of Zion!

David: How can I then allow, that in the middle of
The land of Israel will sit some foreigners,
Like spies, and I should always fear them
And need protection.

Third Emissary: You have no cause to fear them,
Nor any other neighbors.
If threatened – I'd protect you,
The same as I'd protect my own.

David: Your grace is great: you let us live.
But one life, is not equal to another.
An eagle lives and also lives a worm.

First Emissary: Can then the weakling with a strong be same?
The victor and the vanquished?

David: Time weakens the older eagle's wing
And lets the young grow, and be strong.

Second Emissary: It will be bitterness and pain for the young eagle
When he falls in the older eagle's talons!

First Emissary: Enough talking! For the last time we ask:
Are you pulling your army back from the fort?

David: As the hero soldiers who fell by the mountain
Would no more retreat, so

Will not retreat the soldiers who are living!

First Emissary: Words, empty words!
Here you will suffer quick and soon, the
Force of king Akhish. Tremble before his anger!
Remember the fate of King Saul!

(The emissaries leave)

Akhitofel: They will soon raise their army upon us
We will then, need to fight in two campaigns.
Where would we get more forces?
Hence my advice is – to retreat!

David: This is the easiest, and equally, the toughest.
I want to counsel with Yoav, his advice is deft.
We this serious matters we shall wait until the
Morning.
Go in peace Akhitofel.

(Exit Akhitofel)

Ah God! Here I stand with my siege;
To go back, or to advance?
You are my rock and fortress, do not forsake me
Give me a sign!

*(He lies down; it turns dark. soon a figure wearing
A crown on its head shows up)*

King: Forward, forward with fire and sword.
And take over that mountain, the earth around.
It will be your city and in it you'll reside
And there will sit camels laden heavy with treasures
From the land and sea, from Sidon, Amon,
Moab and Aram, and the kings from your house
Making the name of Israel renowned.

*(He disappears, another apparition shows up dressed
in simple attire)*

Prophet: With new force on the fortress advance!
From your clan a branch will spring,
And the world will be blessed with peace,
And never again will fight men with men.
A lion with cattle will graze in peace
And their shepherd will be a child.
All the roads will become one
Up here – at the end of time.

David: *(It is bright and he wakes up)*

Where did the apparitions go?
I see the faces, as if through mist,
But their every word does still remain
And lure and point: embolden me to act!

(Cries)

Your big dream – is taking form! I will again
Storm the fortress of Zion,
And will and must conquer it!
I know that it's no more than a beginning
So I beseech you: in the struggle
With myself and others, in hard times, come again!
Endow me with new strength!
I vow to you: I will offer you
The best powers of my song and life,
Until filled with life anew, and as beautiful
As my dream will be – Jerusalem!

(The last words are accompanied by the trumpeting of Shofars which signal the final storming of the fortress of Zion)

Act III

First scene

(Evening, King David's garden, someone from within the Trees is heard playing. The playing becomes louder, wilder; out, come various groups dancing in pairs)

Jug's full of wine
The harp swaying with sound
So am I – I sing,
Drunk
With desire and lust.

The rock is on fire
The sea stirred by the wind,
And so am I:
With desire and lust.

Lightning spinning high
The snake in the sand –
And so am I:
Shaken I dance,
With desire and lust.

(Amnon and Yonadav enter)

Amnon: That white dress fluttered like a sail
And it is gone, I am that storm and I will
Drive all the sails in the direction that I want.
And if not I'll tear them to pieces.

Yonadav: You rush after too many such sails,
Do not rush to conquer Tamar, or
Her proud brother Avshalom

Will be offended.

Amnon: It's true he is good looking, much better looking
Than I am. But what does Avshalom get from his
Looks? He doesn't know how to conduct himself
With it.

Yonadav: Not only with women he has been successful,
He also knows how to smile to people.

Amnon: I know he lusts to rule the people
While I, for instance, over pretty women.
A pity, he'd come a bit too late,
It's me Amnon – the king's first son
Who will succeed my father's throne!

Yonadav: I'll say again: beware of him!

Amnon: It seems to me that all your talk but serves
That I forget Tamar.
Without some work, you won't succeed!
Nor will you be my counsel
When I become a king.
I need advice on how to get her!

Yonadav: It isn't worth the risk.
Aren't there at court so many others,
Just as beautiful as she?

Amnon: I'm at the court of David
The most licentious of all men,
And Tamar is the most modest
Of all women. Tamar lies in wait and
Irritates me. I want – the most licentious men
To possess the most chaste woman!

Yonadav: Then come, I have devised for you a counsel.

(Yonadav begins to quietly say something to Amnon. They go away. Enter Avshalom and Tamar)

Avshalom: And how are you Tamar, enjoying the holiday?

Tamar: I'm walking around intoxicated and confused.
As if not on firm ground, but carried on a raft.

Avshalom: You should, sister, live more,
You are for sure already a grown girl
How much longer will you hide in little girls'
Rooms and in dreams?

Tamar: When a man casts a glance at me, it feels
As though he'd left a stain on my face.

Avshalom: In the king's court we are the best looking,
If glances from the men chase you
Then glances from the women chase me too.

Tamar: And do you fear the women's glances?

Avshalom: I have no fear of their glances
They are to me, however, all distasteful.
I dream of ruling people, of dominion over
human fates.
I miss the power of a king, more fame; and Amnon,
He will become all that – with effort none.

(In the background show up Amnon and Yonadav)

Amnon: My toil is all for naught! She is with Avshalom!

Yonadav: Since Yonadav devised a ploy,
She's in for a surprise.

(He comes close to Avshalom)

Ah, Minister! From G'shur, from your own

Grandfather, Thalami – a messenger had come.

Avshalom: From grandfather Thalami? Where is he?
Why didn't he come to our court?

Yonadav: The guards won't let a stranger into the city.

Avshalom: A messenger from grandfather is stranger?
I will teach them to behave!

(*To Tamar)*

Forgive me Tamar for leaving you in here; I hope to return soon to the palace.

(Exit Avshalom)

Yonadav: *(Returning to Amnon)*
And now – behold: she's left alone
I'm now redundant; so, off I go.

(Yonadav leaves, Tamar looks at the direction where Avshalom went. After a while, she's slowly commencing to go on the road which leads into the garden; from behind a tree springs out Amnon. She jumps up with fright)

Tamar: Ah, God!

Amnon: Why bring God as an extra partner?
For a guy and a girl, even god is redundant.

Tamar: You Blasphemous Amnon! Not in vain people talk
So much about your deeds.

Amnon: Just as well! Up to your girly rooms
Amnon's course is already well taken!

Tamar: And do you really love all women?

Amnon: Now I love just one – Tamar!

Tamar: *(Draws back alarmed)*

Me? What are you saying?

(Loud music is being played)

Amnon: Ah, Tamar, hear the sound of the harp, the flute,
The cymbals thumping
Calling, begging: come dance, Tamar! Dance with Amnon, Tamar!

Tamar: I dread this game and am afraid of you, of your wild glances,
Let me be back in my room… mother's waiting

Amnon: Do not mention your mother, you're not a child!
Hardly can you frustrate Amnon so.
You are a woman, a ripe woman!

(He pulls her to himself and carries her away in a wild dance, she hangs helplessly in his arms)

I feel the warmth of your body, your virginity, your
Breath, the stiffness of your breast…

Tamar: Amnon! I beseech you,
You should not utter any more such words.
I'm dying… I'm dying of shame…

Amnon: And I – of love!

(He makes a move as if falling)

Tamar: What's with you, Amnon? Amnon! Answer, Amnon!

Amnon: I'm weak… I'm… of too much, is happening…

Tamar: I'll call some people, let me…

Amnon: No! Stay here!
I do not want to spoil the holiday for anyone.
It's noisy… help me… lead me to my room…

(Tamar leads him to the door of his room but she Remains there, standing)

Why are you standing there? Come closer.

Tamar: I'm afraid of you… in your room I have fear…

(Amnon, who all this time was bent, when Tamar led him, straightens up at once, grabs her by the hand, and pulls her into his room. A cry is heard. The doors close and nothing else is heard from there. Enter David.)

David: This picture cannot vanish from my eyes
I thought it was a dream.
I went onto the roof close to the edge
Took a step in the fresh air, and fell down by her feet.
What is it with me? Am I then but a boy
And her – the first woman I see naked?
It is the nature of an older tree,
A barren one to catch a fire fast.
Oh God, don't bring temptation to your servant!

(Enters Akhitofel)

Akhitofel: When all are eating, drinking – happy,
And singing songs, praising the king,
How does the king himself conduct?
He quietly departs from all the guests
And contemplates…

David: I wanted to relieve myself of noise

And went onto the roof.

Akhitofel: And did you find some peace?

David: Yes, peace…

(Abruptly)

Listen, you know of everything. You have people,
Who bring you news from everywhere.
Do you know who lives around my palace?

Akhitofel: I watch your safety and your peace my king,
And it has been my foremost duty, to ensure
That only friends will be your neighbors.

David: And do you know who lives at the house across?

Akhitofel: I know.

David: So tell me.

Akhitofel: Uriah the Hittite.

David: Uriah? Isn't he one of our heroes?

Akhitofel: He is.

David: I think he is with the campaign against Amon.
Who else lives there? His sister?

Akhitofel: No, his wife Batsheva, that is… my granddaughter.

David: Impossible! You – her grandfather?

Akhitofel: What happened to you? Possibly, some misfortune?

David: I just wonder why Batsheva has never shown up
At my house. Batsheva is the wife of one of my heroes

And my happy times are also the happy times of my friends

Akhitofel: You are right my king.
She is a good looking and smart woman
And will surely adorn your court.
Should I go now and bring her over?

David: You can bring Batsheva.

(Exit Akhitofel)

God, what am I doing?
Why did I send to bring her here?
I should right away, call after him,
Overtake him;
He should return and not bring her to me
But my feet – they buckle under,
And my tongue stuck to my pallet!
How quickly he insisted on fetching her to me,
He would have even fetched the devil!

(Enter Akhitofel and Batsheva)

Akhitofel: Here stands by you Batsheva my granddaughter.

Batsheva: (*Kneels)* May the great king David be blessed!

David: Stand up; I would only watch my enemies lie at my feet
The friends, I'd always have them standing by my side.

Batsheva: (*Stands up)* Ah King, I've heard so much about your greatness!

David: You heard stories told about my greatness, but of your Beauty no one needs to tell, I see it plainly.

Akhitofel: (*Makes a motion as if to leave)*

Allow me king…

(David gives him a wink to leave. Akhitofel pretends to leave but instead, he hides himself deep in the garden behind a nearby tree and listen to the conversation)

David: Do you know how beautiful you are, Batsheva?

Bat-Sheva: How rarely have I heard it said!

David: Why rarely? And your man Uriah?

Batsheva: We've known each other still as children
He never got a second wife,
And when I once said this to him:
Uriah, see how comely is my body!
He answered me, as innocent as a child:
Doesn't every woman have such body?

David: I won't deny. I've had a lot of women.
But know this: through all these women
I've only searched for one, just one!

Bat Sheva: And you haven't found the one?

David: I did find the one, once upon a time

Batsheva: Do you mean Mikhal, my king?

David: I see that my life is not unknown to you.

Batsheva: When I was a little child, my mother sang
About your victory over Goliath.
Afterwards, my father too used to tell me of your
Heroic deeds and of your songs.
And once, I remember, when you came from battle
After a victory over the Philistines, I was a child,
Coming to welcome you with flowers I collected,
You took them with thanks and gave me a kiss on my

cheek.
Ah that kiss, until today has been burning in my face.
Do you remember me, that little girl?

David: Forgive me, no. I can't remember.

Batsheva: You see me now for the first time?

David: The second.

Batsheva: And when was the first time?

David: Just now, in your room.

Batsheva: I've been sitting then at home and…

David: Taking a bath.

Batsheva: Whence knows the king?

David: I went for a stroll on the roof,
And saw from there how you were bathing
How beautiful, how magnificent is your body,
Batsheva!

Batsheva: Is it prettier than other women that you've known?

David: Prettier, much prettier!

Batsheva: Oh God!

David: I have known so many pretty women,
But really loved: only the first.
It is Saul who tore her away from me
And when we joined again,
We faced each other just like strangers.
Since then the years have ambled on,
Hard, with wars and worries.
I have grown old and thought that in my heart

Turned off forever the last spark of love
But now, when I beheld you bathing, I felt
That in my heart rekindled,
The flame of my young years.
I know that for certain: the last love,
Is equal to the first.

Batsheva: Speak… Speak more…

David: I feel now that you are the present
The last, which gives me life.
The sun in the month of Sivan, what does it mean?
In autumn day how love is ours in each precious
Ray of light.

Batsheva: I love autumn… it is the time of ripeness and fruit

David: So come to enjoy its abundance…

*(He leaves with Batsheva, Akhitofel comes out
From behind the tree)*

Akhitofel: Aha! How well I've managed this affair!
What flaming lusty eyes he cast upon her!
He is forever captive of Batsheva!
Through her I'll gain more power than them all!
You Yoav, will take a fortress from a foe,
By staging siege for many weeks;
After battle hard, and blood aplenty
By tens of thousands hero men:
But I, to win, need no more than one woman
And she is readily at hand!

(*Exit Akhitofel, Enter Tamar)*

Tamar: Alas! Where should I now back into,
And where would I conceal my shame?
I'm fed up with my looks!

How could I now put on a snow-white dress
On my violated body?

(Starts to tear up her dress)

So! I will tear it now to pieces!
And put ashes on my head!

(Sinks down weakly, Enter Batsheva)

Batsheva: Now go home Bat-Sheva, quietly… quietly…
And shall no eye, no stranger notice you
Batsheva, are you the same as before?
Will you walk in the street, and people
Look at you like always? No one will know
That for you down on his knees knelt – the powerful,
The great king David, and your mouth,
Made his lips tremble!
And in your arms he was in heat and fever
stammering.
Till now the greater battle-victory hasn't given
Me such happiness and pleasure.

(Takes a few steps back)

I will lock up myself in my room
And there, preserve each part, give in;
For every happiness and pleasure spend my life
Meanwhile Batsheva quietly… quietly… quietly…

*(She hastily retreats out of the garden but suddenly
Stops and listens. From somewhere nearby she hears
A low groan.)*

It seems to me, someone is groaning here?

Tamar: People… people…

Batsheva: *(Notices Tamar lying on the ground)*

A woman? What is going on with you? Who are you?

Tamar: Do not ask me who I am, but better ask who I once was.
Because right now I'm shame itself, misery, despair!

Batsheva: Your hair disheveled eyes — welled up, your dress is torn
And crumpled. Answer me! What happened to you girl?

Tamar: It was Amnon who with force had taken me…

Batsheva: Why with force? Why didn't you agree?

Tamar: I have dreamed of a man noble and tender
Who for years won't even dare to touch me.
So he came, taking me by force without a kiss
Without a gentle word…

Batsheva: What are you stammering for, my lost child?
It is a good man who is timely and experienced
Who knows how to appreciate our beauty.

Tamar: Who are you to speak so unshamed?
You are sin itself!

Batsheva: What are you crying for?
You want everyone to know what happened?

Tamar: Let it be known to the street, the city, the country –
The whole world!
May they all be violated as I was! The flowers and the
Trees the rivers and the mountains, and in the heavens all
the stars!
Then all the trees will be denuded of their leaves
Just as I was ashamed and naked!
And may the flowers close their petals,
The mountains slide into the valleys from despair
The stars extinguish for all time!

(Runs away)

Batsheva: She cries. To many more that man will bring misfortune
But you Batsheva, with your received happiness – slink
Quietly… quietly…

(Slinks away. Enter David)

David: I've heard crying from within the garden.
And it seemed like a voice of a woman.
Did the guards detain her, and did she
Cry because of them?

(Cries)

Who Cried? Indeed there comes no answer.
Apparently, this I've just imagined.
But no! I hear some steps. There's someone there!

(Enters Avshalom)

What are you doing now there in the garden Avshalom?
Did you meet someone on the road?

Avshalom: A woman. I've met a woman here before!

David: And how did the woman look?

Avshalom: Disheveled!

David: Avshalom, silence!

Avshalom: I can't be silent!

David: Quiet!

Avshalom: And would that have been a commoner instead
The crown would still not tolerate it.

David: Remember Avshalom, that I am your father!

Avshalom: You can choose! Either you are the father of
Tamar and Avshalom,
Or you are the father of Amnon!

David: I… I do not understand you. What are you saying?

Avshalom: Do you know what happened to Tamar?

David: I know nothing.

Avshalom: Amnon lured her to his room and there he raped her.

David: And it was she, who cried?

Avshalom: It was she.

David: Avshalom, take her to your house to sit there
And wait till all calms down.

Avshalom: And when will you punish Amnon?

David: About this, I indeed will have to think.

Avshalom: Because of a woman once dishonored
Our people once declare a war and
Nearly killed a whole tribe!

David: Should I, because of your sister,
Kill the house of David?

Avshalom: Amnon is not the entire house of David!

David: You don't know everything! With kings it
Often happens that along with their great deeds
They also do injustice,
They often go together hand in hand.

Avshalom: A king should hold himself as an example.

David: You have never been a king
And for you, this life did not unlock
The wide doors to experience.
It could so happen:
Should you encounter such affair,
Woe upon you if the people wanted
To punish you,
As harshly as you wished to punish them.

Avshalom: And so, Amnon will not be punished?

David: He won't escape the punishment.
But I will find the time and method, so be patient.

(Exit David)

Avshalom: And I – I will not wait with patience!
I will myself exact revenge from him.
And who will be now David's Eldest son and heir?
Rejoice my heart! It is no more a dream:
The king of Israel will be – Avshalom!

Second scene

(Jerusalem, in David's house,
David, Batsheva)

David: Pardon me Bat-Sheva, weeks ago
I got from you a message, that
You're pregnant, I haven't called you
For so many feverish thoughts I had
Looking for solution for us both.

Batsheva: I have indeed for years, hoped, dreamed,
To feel the start of a child in me,
Why can't I now be free?

David: I have decided to call him in.

Batsheva: Who?

David: Your husband. It's already three days since he came

Batsheva: He probably knows why he is here!

David: He knows of nothing.

Batsheva: What is the reason that he hasn't seen me?

David: He said: if Yoav and his army are
In Amon on the battlefield and suffering from the heat
And from the arrows of their enemy,
He will not go home to his wife, and won't relax.

Batsheva: Oh God! Where did he sleep the
Last three nights?

David: With my servants in my house

Batsheva: And he didn't even want to see me?

David: And possibly you wanted to see him?

Batsheva: Heavens forbid!
After that, I have nothing to say to him.

(Enter Akhitofel)

Akhitofel: I am bringing bad, dark news:
Avshalom had killed Amnon!

David: My son Amnon let me see my Amnon!

Akhitofel: Did you hear?

Batsheva: A cruel Avshalom!

Akhitofel: I believe that robbing a man of his honor
Is more than robbing him of his life –
It was indeed Amnon that raped his sister
You're quiet? I know that this concerns you too.
Uriah is in town. When he finds out…

Batsheva: And do you also know that *he* betrayed *me*?

Akhitofel: You must be joking with me Batsheva
Did he betray you on the battlefield?

Batsheva: Not on the battlefield, but with the battlefield.
He's been here for three days and hasn't shown himself.
You would call that bravery and strength,
But I – I call it cowardice and weakness.
I want a man, for whom, not the king
And not the people, but *I* will be the first.
He thinks I must be his forever.
A woman wins a man not in a battle
Men must for her continuously struggle.
If I had found him coming, I would have

Fallen to his tired feet and washed them
With my tears; and, not even as his wife
But as his slave, I would have stayed for
My entire life.
But he remembered everyone:
The king, his people and Yoav
But not Batsheva.
Now our account is balanced:
For I betray him with the king
And he betrays me with the king.

Akhitofel: And aren't you shamed to face the people?

Batsheva: Surely wives will gossip about me
Not of godliness but from envy.

Akhitofel: And if you have no shame in you
Will I have to bear the cost myself?

Batsheva: I don't want you talking of it anymore.
It isn't right to lament dawn, when the sun
Replaces morning stars.

Akhitofel: You are dreaming. The sun is still under the clouds!

Batsheva: For David's love it is worthwhile to cede a kingdom
But to Batsheva David's love will *give* a kingdom!

(Exit Batsheva)

Akhitofel: When I let Batsheva into David's house,
I was next to her: instructing her that she
Forever should be grateful
And strive on my behalf with David
But she – what impudence! – Had answered
That she will not in the least abide!
You are the smallest thing for the king's love!
David bought Uriah's loyalty
David bought Batsheva's love,

But Akhitofel's brain he lost!
And without my brain, for wise David it will be
Difficult to rule; but with my brain,
Avshalom the fool – could also be a King!

(Exit Akhitofel, Enter David)

David: No time enough to mourn Amnon,
And Uriah is already waiting.
I shall with him attempt to talk.
Ah, God! Soften up your heart so that I wouldn't
Have to cover up one sin with a much bigger one.

(He leaves and returns with Uriah)

Uriah, I summoned you from Amon,
Months ago from the battlefield so you
May use the rest you earned,
But you have stubbornly declared
That you won't rest, when the army is in battle.
That shows that you are loyal, and I have decided
To safeguard the life of a loyal man
You will be from today at the head of my own guard.

Uriah: Do forgive my king. Since my childhood
I have been reared a soldier, tough and simple.
Even to my wife, to my Batsheva,
It is hard for me to utter
A warm word, a gentle loving word where
You should utter wise and pretty words —
Conduct yourself with gentleness – better send me
Back there where I am needed – to the war.

David: *(Thinks for a while)*

You can return to the army.

Uriah: I will go, like an arrow off a bow!

David: A moment! Say Uriah; are you really loyal to me?

Uriah: With your name on my lips,
I throw myself in the greatest battlefield danger.

David: And if you heard that I have sinned?

Uriah: I'd strike down who ever dared to say that!

David: And if you found it to be true?

Uriah: I dread to even think it.

David: Think of it and answer.

Uriah: For me you are the most heroic and greatest king.
With that thought – I can rest in peace.
In rain and in heat, in hunger and thirst
And destroy an entire city, and therefore
With this thought I, too, can be myself a hero!

David: And if doubt came to your mind?

Uriah: I'd stab myself for daring so to dwell!

David: *(Jumps off his throne)*

That is too much!

(Sits back, and thinks for a while)

I will give you a letter for Yoav.

(Writes a letter and gives it to Uriah)

You should safeguard it closely.

Uriah: If I lose it – I pay with my life. *(Exit Uriah)*

David: And there he goes – paying with his life!

(He goes to the door at the right and calls)

Batsheva!

(Enters Batsheva)

Uriah has left.

Batsheva: And how did you dismiss him?

David: I thought that I could talk to him
As one man to another.
A man should understand a manly weakness,
But when he spoke to me just like a soldier,
He forced me to be – just a king.
And a soldier is ought to be able
To be sacrificed for me, the same as I
Sacrifice for the people of Israel.

Batsheva: Uriah wants to be loyal to king David.
The king wants to be loyal to the people of Israel
And I Batsheva, should I be loyal to none?
A king and a hero lay over the burden of fate
On a weaker woman!

David: I carry, just like you, the cloud of Uriah
But, with you I'm ready, more to bear:
For God and people – the regret and shame
My part as husband and as king will be much harder…

Act IV

First Scene

(A street in Hebron, Akhitofel comes in)

Akhitofel: Quite often David has complained to me,
That I am too brainy, limited and sober
With no imagination.
And Yoav: that I am neither bold nor brave;
I will surprise them both and they shall see
That they are indeed, mistaken.
I dared! I've started now a thing, that
If it won't succeed, I'll pay for it with my own head.
And Akhitofel's head – is worth a treasure.
I've tied a bond with Avshalom
To make a stand against the king;
If indeed, Yoav will be a friend of Avshalom,
There will also be peace between Yoav and David
He will certainly ensure that comes a time,
When Avshalom,
The crown inherits, and is king
He will stay the leader of the army.
Aha! I have destroyed his plans,
Avshalom is now falling off their hands,
And is in mine, in mine!
I've never had a hope to gain in power
From King David's hands
Because his ways lead to the war, but
For conducting wars, he doesn't need me
But Yoav and his brave men.
But I shall rule, next to Avshalom!
He's got long and pretty curls
But has no head. His head is Akhitofel!
Here he comes.

(Enter Avshalom)

Avshalom: Do you still hold, Akhitofel that the

Uprising should begin, not in Jerusalem…

Akhitofel: I still maintain my old opinion as before:
That it is safer to begin here in Hebron.
In Jerusalem David has a lot of friends and brave men
And your honor is not here reduced:
It is here, indeed, that David was anointed.

Avshalom: You may be right, but tell me now:
Is your resolve not lessened?
He's been your friend for years…

Akhitofel: And he has been until this day – your father.
Lose me, and you still are David's son…
And can expect your father's grace,
But I – I risk my honor and my life.

Avshalom: We risk nothing because we win.

(A blowing of the shofar is heard)

You hear? My men are blowing the shofar
And summoning the people to the streets.

(People enter)

1st person: What's going on? What does the blowing of the shofar mean?

2nd person: Are we under attack from our enemies?

3rd person: I swear it's David's son, it's Avshalom!

4th person: And do you know who's next to him?
It's Akhitofel!

5th person: What are these great ministers doing here?

3rd person: Probably they're bringing up something important!

2nd person: We should get closer so we can hear well.

Avshalom: As an old sailor looks at the storm clouds
Over the sea – I am drunk when I see these people surge.

Akhitofel: And especially in a storm, it is forbidden to be
Drunk… one should calmly be at the helm.

Avshalom: If so – then you speak first.

Akhitofel: Residents of Hebron – friends and brothers!
You all certainly know of, and can appreciate
The great deeds of King David.
He unified the people of Israel
And freed us from the yoke of our enemies.
Therefore long live King David!

People: Long live, long live king David!

Akhitofel: But the victories first came
After long, hard, bloody wars.
And who amongst you did not lose
Your kin, your father, brother?
Pretty soon, the whole nation of Israel
Will become a nation of widows and orphans!
Is it all so that you can have nice houses
While your beloved, gentle children
Lie always in the fields
In the heat, the wind and rain?
Is that so that you'd have vineyards and grapes?
When your beloved blessed children
Languidly expire in the deserts?
You should be given time and also rest
So that you enjoy the victories.
Enough wars! We need peace, peace!

People: Enough wars! We need peace, peace!

Akhitofel: As Long as Yoav leads the army
It won't be possible for you to rest.
He agitates and drives continuously for war
So he can gain fame as a hero.

People: Away with Yoav! We want peace!

Akhitofel: However, Yoav's not alone and without help;
He is supported by others, and the soldiers
All with things to gain:
They helped David in his wanderings
When he was fleeing Saul,
Surely David should be grateful,
But should he always give them
An office in the kingdom?
So many youth have grown up,
No small number of them, bold and able
There are a lot of them I'm certain,
Even here among you in Hebron.
Therefore I pronounce: power to the young!

Young voices: Power to us! Power to the young!

Akhitofel: How does a man conduct himself in life?
King David is too strongly bound with Yoav
And also with the hero soldiers.
Many times Avshalom tried, and I did too,
Occasionally, to separate the king from them
But our labors always were to no avail.
It seems to me that David's not their master
But their slave.

(Murmuring among the people)

But David's not to blame,
He is already old and weak, and needs a man
Who can assist him:
But who'll assist him you will ask,

And who's astute and just?
Not Yoav, not Yoav's brother Avishay,
Nor any of the hero warriors.
There is only one in Israel,
It's Avshalom!

Voices: Long live Avshalom!

Akhitofel: Here stands for you Avshalom himself…
So look at him, at his form and face,
And his long wonderful locks of hair –
This is a young lion, no other will
Compare to him in beauty! And not only he is handsome
But also righteous, he fears no one,
Even to sternly punish a brother, when he's done
A loathsome thing.
And need a man have a good extraction,
Could he match with Avshalom?
His father is a king and his mother too
Is a daughter of a king.
Therefore, let everybody call with me together:
Long live Avshalom our king!

Voices from the people: Long live Avshalom our king!

(After that a suspicious whispering)

Avshalom: *(To Akhitofel, upset)* did you hear?

Akhitofel: And also for them I have a solution.

(Calls out)

Does anyone disagree?

(Quiet)

Jerusalem is already for Avshalom,

Jericho, Giva'a, Ramah, Gilgal, Mitspah –
Do you want to be an exception?

People: Long live Avshalom our king!

Second Scene

(David's house in Jerusalem, David and Yoav. Enter Khushay)

Khushay: We have barely managed crossing through the crowds,
That like a torrid thorn-bush fill the streets.
I haven't recognized many of the people, that
Would always greet me with their friendship –
Only foreign, insolent and hostile miens.
I heard cries against the king, which made the blood
In my own veins — flush my countenance – for shame.

David: What does the crowd demand?
Speak clearly now Khushay.

Khushay: Avshalom is rebelling against you.
First did Hebron go to him, next,
Many other cities joined,
And soon it will be your Jerusalem!

Yoav: Give, my king, the order to attack the plotters
With our army!

David: I want to consult with Akhitofel.

Khushay: He became Avshalom's right hand man!

David: Ah God! Destroy all his plans!
I have resolved to only battle with my neighbors
And lost this land to Akhitofel.

He fed me with false information,
And other knowledge, from me he totally concealed.

Khushay: An exposed traitor is better than
A hidden one. It is a useful revolution:
It tells you who's your friend, and who's your foe
It cleans and purifies your world.

Yoav: I admit, I was the one who for Avshalom pleaded
And conciliated between you both.
I will pay for that mistake my king. With all my forces
I will throw myself against him, and spare no
Sacrifice; the army is with us and we shall win.

David: A battlefield victory is enough to dominate a foreign and
Hostile people, but not enough to win them over,
Therefore I order:
Call together all of those who are still loyal to the king
Because we soon desert Jerusalem.

Yoav: You want to hand him over the city itself?
I won it in a hard battle
And won't lose it without a fight.

David: You have lived continuously to conquer cities
Be ready now to give one up.

(Yoav silent)

Are you too, against me?

Yoav: You have commanded!

(Yoav leaves)

David: Do you hear, do you hear the noise, the crying?
What else do they want from King David?
What didn't I do for the people of Israel?
I have freed them from the yoke of strangers

I have unified the tribes into one nation
And built the city of Jerusalem –
A fortress for the state and God!

Khushay: Forgive me but I think that you continuously,
Have occupied yourself with preparations for the future
And for the present gave but small consideration.
You have thought about the people as a whole
And often overlooked the individual.

David: I think otherwise.
Those who in the sea – observe just drops
See neither sea nor drops.
Those who in the flame see but the sparks
They neither see a flame nor spark –
In the people, I only want to see the greater whole
And in a day – what shall remain for generations.
I've always called upon the people and
Drove them for renewal
So now came Akhitofel and Avshalom,
And with false and gentle words
Leading far from this ideal.
But I haven't in the people, lost all hope!
Does the sea forget its own importance,
And escapes while there's an outlet?
The first thing I should do – is wait it out
Gather all of those remaining loyal.
Time is of the essence!

(To a servant by the door)

Rush on Yigli,
And call here Queen Ma'akha!

(Servant leaves)

Do you consider Khushay, going with me?

Khushay: I am not Akhitofel, his friendship for you, was his office

Probably Avshalom gave him a higher office,
So he soon betrayed you.
My friendship is free and true to the king!

David: I should have people by Avshalom, who will
Disrupt his plans. Against Akhitofel I have to
Place such a man who in wisdom is his match
And is also true and loyal, there is such a man
And it is Khushay.

(Enter Ma'akha)

Ma'akha: What is happening, why have you summoned me in haste?

David: Something extraordinary has happened.

Ma'akha: Is it, God forbid, bad news?

David: For me it hit severely,
For you, I wish to see.

Ma'akha: How can it be that the same news
Could make me happy, and you sad?

David: So hear: Avshalom had started a revolt, and
He is after the crown, and his father's head.

Ma'akha: Oh God have mercy!

David: I decided for now, to abandon Jerusalem
I'm taking along, those who would share with me my fate.

Ma'akha: Oh, Avshalom, my son!

David: Time is short, you must decide, Ma'akha.
Whether you go with the men, or, on the contrary,
Stay with your son?

Ma'akha: Unhappy mother me!
Two children I do have: Tamar and Avshalom.
Shining from the heavens,
Avshalom, bright and flaming like the sun.
And Tamar – soft and dainty like the moon.
When Amnon, with aggression stained her honor
I thought at least, I will find consolation
In my only son, in Avshalom.
So he himself now stains his own honor!

David: They are Ma'akha, indeed my children too
But when Tamar was shamed, she kept her
Shame in her own room.
Avshalom dragged his shame outdoors,
For the entire people of Israel to see.
What I had forgiven Amnon as a father
I cannot forgive Avshalom as king.

Ma'akha: Children always leave their mothers
And for her love they pay her – with estrangement
The husband stays until his life is done.
I have decided; I go with you together.

David: I thank you Ma'akha, go now to your room.
And pick the things you need the most.
I will not make our way more difficult with burden.

(Ma'akha leaves, enters Yoav and the ministers)

You ministers and heroes, friends and warriors!
I believe that you, who are now with me
Through the fleeting years, did not preserve your
Strength or blood so that the people of
Israel should be the kind of people
Who are enslaved by foreigners,
You will not save your power to forestall
Your freedom.
We have given up our lives,
To make Israel big and strong.

Now when we stand at the eve of our fulfillment,
Will we abandon all of our accomplishment
To traitors and deceivers?
Not only *I*, am asking you right now,
But future generations ask you too!

Yoav: We feel that there is only but one answer:
Death to the traitors! Long live King David!

All: Death to the traitors, long live king David!

David: And now, you, who remained loyal to me
And picked a course the same as mine –
Our scabbards, from today will never be apart
Joining me on this far and thorny road.

Third scene

(In the forest, Avshalom's tent. Avshalom and Amasah)

Avshalom: Amasah, what do the spies say?

Amasah: They have confirmed that David's army
Is much smaller than our own.

Avshalom: Like a mighty frothing cloud
We shall wash the enemy off the land.
Amasah, we're done, we have prepared enough,
We will not wait a moment more –
Let the battle start!

Amasah: The battle has begun!

(Leaves)

Avshalom: I'm feverishly awaiting our victory
Early on this evening I will really be
The king of all of Israel!

(A veiled woman shows up at the tent. Avshalom steps back)

Who are you?

(She unveils her face)

Mother of mine!

Ma'akha: My Avshalom!

Avshalom: How did you get to me?

Ma'akha: From David's camp I clandestinely stole away.
A slave had led me through some savage roads
With danger lurking on each side,
But I still managed to come through.

Avshalom: You have done well to run from him.
You shall remain here till the end of war
Thereafter you will sit with me together
In Jerusalem In the palace of the king.

Ma'akha: I will sit in the king's palace, not just with you
But also with King David.

Avshalom: He has no place for us together!
And David's got already many wives beside you.

Ma'akha: But I have just one husband and it's David.

Avshalom: And a son you also have just one.

Ma'akha: I should therefore abandon neither one!

Avshalom: There can only be one king in Israel!

Ma'akha: So the one that's there – there he should stay.
Avshalom, aren't your hair-locks
More beautiful than the prettiest crown?
The crown that sways you now, against a father
And tomorrow – against the people,
Could later even sway you – against God himself.
I have for many years known David's life:
His body was a field in drought.
Hail – would fall on him when it wanted
Locust – would smite him when it pleased
And when Yoav faraway conducted war
He lay awake and restless through the night
And you Avshalom in the middle of a summer
Are lean and handsome, and tender and refined,
Need to drink wine and be merry and dance
And bask in the love of pretty women
And each day ask of God
That he might prolong your father's life
So that he can sit on his old chair
And rest his tired limbs
So that you could for many, many years
Feel happy and enjoy it all.

Avshalom: Forgive me, mother, I desire neither wine nor dance,
And no pretty women, all I want is power!

Ma'akha: Is it sweeter than wine? Prettier than women,,
More enjoyable than dance?

Avshalom: Yes! It's sweeter, prettier, more enjoyable!

Ma'akha: And dearer than your parents?

Avshalom: Dearer!

Ma'akha: Oh God, what kind of words are these,
I could never understand their meaning!

Avshalom: The meaning of the words is that I am a man!

Ma'akha: It is a pity that I don't have only daughters
But I remember when you were a child,
A dainty, shy, and soft and quiet
Hiding deep eyes, with long hair.
When you walked with Tamar
Everyone thought: they are sisters.

Avshalom: And also when I grew much older,
I've heard it being said a lot!
I am, however, not a woman! David
Never took me with him to the war;
I have hands too weak to hold a sword,
I am too frail for heat and rain.
Enough! No more marveling at my looks –
Men should tremble at my sight.
I will make my resolve, seen by everyone.
I have slept with my father's wives
And will wrestle away the crown from him
by force!
And for you, who came to make me weakling
In my heart awakens pity
I ought to say to you: you are mistaken!

Ma'akha: I leave, disregarding your reproof and whining,
All the more still seeing you,
As a stubborn child who wants to show
His parents that he's bigger.

Avshalom: After the battle you shall see that
I am great!

Ma'akha: Who knows? It could be, that then, your mother
Will find out.

(Exit Ma'akha, Enter Akhitofel)

Akhitofel: See now how correct was my advice:

I had advised to chase immediately
After David, while he was wandering.
But he liked more, Khushay's advice
And by then discovered that:
David had gathered a whole army.

Avshalom: I suppose that Khushay has for that an answer,
I will summon him.

Akhitofel: My efforts are for naught!
I'd looked for him all over camp
And haven't found him.
Like a snake, Khushay had let his poison out
And he is gone.

Avshalom: May he be forever cursed!

Akhitofel: And how did you pick such a traitor for a counsel?

Avshalom: I am not wiser than King David:
His counsel is a traitor just as well …

Akhitofel: You are correct. I have earned the ridicule
When I exchanged David with you
And put my fate in your hands.

Avshalom: Don't brag; for me you're only one,
I have a lot more like you in Israel!

Akhitofel: That is nothing but a crowd
Which stands with you unhappy.
That is too lazy to work and think
But not too lazy to disrupt and to destroy.

Avshalom: You blaspheme me and my loyal men
I will therefore punish you severely!

Akhitofel: I'm not afraid of you, for I have anyway –
Already everything forfeited!

(Enter Amasah)

Amasah: We've been defeated!
Run away! Save yourselves!

Avshalom: But that's not possible at all!
You know our army is much bigger!

Amasah: They attacked us from three sides,
Our camp is torn and beaten!

Avshalom: We shall fight on! I myself, the king
Will lead the army into battle!

Amasah: Too late!

Avshalom: Obey me – or I'll strike you down!

(Pulls out his sword)

Amasah: I go!

(Exit Avshalom and Amasah)

Akhitofel: His fear has given him wings.
But they won't stay afloat much longer.
He has forfeited, and I – along with him.
I've left him plenty of my wisdom
But wisdom's not enough. Wisdom without love
And without faith – is blind.
My name will be for generations held
For shame and mockery as traitor
Even my children and my children's children
Will be followed by disgrace and shame.
Not Akhitofel is my name but Akhitofet!*

(Takes out a rope)

---

* Literally: brother from hell

Ah, Linden tree, I have a request, a last one –
For a bond. Give me here a branch for hanging.
Forgive me if the branch will wither soon,
Or, if on it birds won't sing,
Just cranes will be its visitors –
The request from a traitor, though his last.

(Ties the rope to a branch)

Soon the great wise man, Akhitofel
Will be the greatest hanging foolish corpse.

(Hangs himself. Enter Avshalom)

Avshalom: Where are you my ministers, my warriors? –
Run away and leave the king alone!
Where from did David get so quickly
So many soldiers, in his tiny camp?
No others than lions and tigers
With David's army fought against us.
Ah, mole let me in your burrow hide,
Just like you I want to crawl into the ground!
Ah, sun – go under, maybe the clouds
Will hide me, protect me from danger!

*(He suddenly sees Akhitofel hanging. He lets out a cry
And runs away)*

I am afraid of death! I will not die.

Fourth scene

(At David's court, David and Khushay)

David: With Akhitofel, I often used to counsel
And sometimes with Yoav confer,

But seldom turned to you.
At first, in our wretchedness, in our wanders
When I sent you to Avshalom –
For the first time I had felt
How necessary it is even for a king,
To have a friend with whom he can confide.
Oh say, you came from Avshalom's
And met there with his people,
(Not all are simply just plain traitors)
What moved them to betray me?

Khushay: I think, my king, you are forgetting,
That Israel is not an ancient realm,
Such as Egypt; for many generations
The people there have been accustomed
To a king, and their king is even like a God.
Israel was used to judges,
Who were ever present,
And for them not being saved from hatred
Was just enough of a consolation.
Saul who then became a king,
Had too, until his death, remained a man of the people.
But you – you've had repeated victories
Gained outside the borders of Israel.
You believed that if you'd triumph over strangers
You would surely gain the favor of the people
But only then, when in the street, in front of crowds,
You danced, in front of the holy ark –
You won their love,
Much more, then with your greatest winning battle.

David: In my wanders often came,
These thoughts harassing me
It's not how *you* would say it
But I would often think of that,
I'd wish to rule some foreign nations
But long before I won over our people of Israel
I'd wanted just to rule them,
And long before that, I won over my family.

But if I'm safely home:
From many nations – I come to Israel
From kingship – to my family,
And from an advisor to a friend.
For there cannot be a greater triumph
Than to be embraced by love
Of your own people, your own woman
Child and friend.

Slave: *(Jumps in with a cry)*

Dear me! Queen Ma'akha poisoned herself!

David: Ah, Ma'akha, Ma'akha!

(Jumps out and comes back immediately with Ma'akha In his hands)

Say, what happened?
Why did you poison yourself, Ma'akha, answer!

Ma'akha: I dread the end of the war…
I want to see neither you, nor Avshalom dead in shackles…
I shall die first…
(Dies)

David: How hard it is without you Ma'akha, to go on living.
Should a defeat befall me – I could muster strength
And courage to endure.
But if I am victorious, how could I as father triumph
When the vanquished is my son?

(Enter a messenger)

Messenger: Victory! Victory! Victory!

David: And what is the news of Avshalom my son?

Messenger: An end befitting all of those who hate the King!

David: My son Avshalom!

(Enter Yoav)

Yoav: King David, You have won!

David: My son, my son Avshalom!

Yoav: The warriors have won for you
Much blood was shed and your crown secured
They have now gathered by the house
To receive your greetings.

David: My son Avshalom!

Yoav: It was not the case of son and father,
It was a case involving all the people.

David: The first right of judgment is the father's

Yoav: He killed Amnon his brother, and you forgave him,
I then believed him too, and spoke to you on his behalf.
The first time, he took me for a fool,
But now, his sentence had to come.
Greet them for your victory!

David: My son Avshalom!

Yoav: And if you will not greet this army,
I will go out and instantly declare,
That David will no more be king!

Khushay: It's not only Yoav; the warriors want to see you too.

David: I will greet them.

Yoav: *(Opens a window, cries to the army)*

King David is happy, and will thank you for your victory!

David: *(Stands between Yoav and Khushay)*

I thank you… I greet you for your victory… I'm happy…

(Falls in Khushay's arms)

Yoav: *(Yells down to the soldiers)*

Long live King David!

Soldiers: Long live! Long live King David!

Act V

First scene

(In David's court, Mikhal, Batsheva)

Batsheva: From day to day I feel more drawn to you
We are not similar in looks or spirit,
We are, though, just the same, oddly connected!
You are the first wife of King David,
And I – the last. You and I – we are
The circle that locks David's life.
But while you knew him at his start, as a young man,
Glowing with song and love,
I only knew him – constantly engaged in war,
Sick and tired, with worries for his kingdom.

Mikhal: My fate is not much better than is yours.
It's much like that of a tree.

It turns green in spring but soon it is denuded,
Sadly, through the summer.
Of springtime we have nothing left
Like the faded blood of memories.

Batsheva: I have indeed encountered David early in his autumn.

Mikhal: Autumn's filled with blessings,
The time of fruitfulness – you had a child!

Batsheva: I have a son, wise and good looking,
But David's very sick; what would befall
Me and my son should he expire?
They scorn us both, all of David's wives:
Of you they're jealous, for you are a daughter of king
Saul and you out rank them.
But me they hate, for they maintain
That I came here through sin, and David has been
Paying for that instant for too long.

Mikhal: Why are you worried, and do not talk to all the other wives?

Batsheva: Everybody thinks the same.
As soon as David dies, Shlomo and I will have no guard,
And be exposed to everybody's mockery and indignations.
Haven't I for that sin paid enough?
My child, the first I had, is dead
And through the night, in sleep I see Uriah:
He doesn't cry, not even open his mouth –
He just disrobes himself, showing me his breast,
Pierced by an arrow, so bloodied, bloody…
I wake each night, crying and lamenting, drenched
In sweat and lie in agony and fright till dawn.

Mikhal: I gage love, not only with pleasure
That is willing to give or take,
But with a measure of misery and sacrifice

In which it is therefore, ready to partake.
You have been victimized and sacrificed
Therefore, you can proudly come to David
Requesting and demanding that which you deserve.
I hear him coming. Speak to him once more.
I long for… I ache so much to see his face.
To hear his voice, but I shouldn't and I can't…

Batsheva: Allow me my king,

David: Speak, Batsheva, I hear you,

Batsheva: Forgive me, that even though you're sick, I came
And would knowingly disturb your peace.
I have resolved that every moment is so dear.
You're certainly aware, I haven't wavered,
When you first brought me in here,
And was devoted to you from the start.
I then had listened to the voice,
Strong female voice inside me, that for years
Had been ashamed and never heard, but
Set my heart on fire while
You were far conducting wars
When in the house I stayed alone,
And quietly consumed by flames.

David: Would you have rather not become my wife?

Batsheva: How curt! Don't forget I soon became a mother,
Since that earlier child of ours died, I took it as a
punishment, and when Shlomo, our second, came
I was drawn, the more to love him,
Protect him from the lightest wind, that the littlest
Bird, heaven forbid, won't peck at him, and seven times
At night I went to see — how he sleeps and how he
breaths.
I also haven't seen how every spring the earth turns
green,
While I myself, don't care for jewelry and clothes – I

had been
Just a mother. And while I sacrificed a lot for being mother –
I come here in your name, and ask that our son will be your heir.

David: But Shlomo is the youngest.

Batsheva: Life and death hang in the balance!

David: I see that Shlomo can have better life without a crown.

Bat-Sheva: They give him wine and let him sing
And freely speak. When he likes, of what he likes.
While you are still around, while all know that
You love him, and are willing to protect him,
If it's found that he committed an injustice.
But if, God forbid, you weren't there
Then, they would pounce on him like wolves.
Because they do not tolerate one, such as Shlomo,
That sits in a tavern proud as king.
And, were he king, would feel as happy,
Just as he is in a tavern.
Of such they know not in their midst,
They only know of vagrants or of kings.

David: You know how much I love Shlomo.
If only I could find some extra time,
I would have called him to my side
I could have found in him the traces,
Of my childhood, and my youth.
(I've found a lot of that in him by now)
There is between us, though, a great divide:
My father was Yishay the peasant,
And his father is King David. I – have fought and
Suffered to get what's mine, and he – is winning by inheritance;
Therefore he doesn't know its value.

Batsheva: I don't deny it: he doesn't know of worries and of burden,
And these, sometimes, suffice to thwart so much
By disappointment, that he could suddenly transform his life.

David: It won't be me who now will bring him disappointment…
And though I can now call him – go and fetch him here to me.

Batsheva: I thank you, my king.

(Exit Batsheva, Enter Yoav)

Yoav: How are you dealing with your sickness, king ?

David: None better, I had thought:
After stamping out Avshalom's rebellion,
I will overcome and start a new life.
I have, however, fallen into illness, and I see
That I don't have much time left,
To get ready for my death.

Yoav: You can rest calm,
You have a good heir – Adoniyah.
I prepared him. He's my loyal pupil.
I teach him how to fence with swords
And also how to shoot his arrow to the target.
He frequently consults with me, and wants to know
Of your heroic deeds and battles.
And when I start to tell him –
He listens eager and amazed.
He swears by God to follow in your footsteps,
Neither right nor left, not to stray from them,
Not even one step off.

David: You are mistaken.
What does he want? – Two times David is impossible!

A young man should explore a course,
That fits him and his time anew,
Will he be waging wars with neighbors?
Did Avshalom's strength that drew to him
So many people bring him peace?
The truth is that he did not give them peace, but bloody war.
Therefore, bringing peace is harder than conducting war.
I should therefore ensure, that our people have a king who's wise,
Who truly will, by force, bring rest and peace.

Yoav: And if the neighbors realize,
That our army's gotten weaker,
Do you suppose, that they would then
Continue to pay tribute and be meek?

David: I am in doubt,
And further, I can now confess to you,
That once I had big plans.
I had a dream: to subjugate all of our neighbors
And since that long, so long ago, to make
Our borders wider through aggression…
But I am old and gotten sick and cannot see it through.
Should my heir not stretch the borders – he should
At least protect them.
And hear: I think the lot of Israel is
Already drawn: not to rule with power,
But with soul!

Yoav: It's not enough, it's not enough!
When Saul had lost his final battle,
Didn't also then, the Holy-Ark fall
To the hands of our foes?

David: And even if I would have, already granted
Your design – who'd have the force to see it through?

Yoav: Adoniyah.

And even if he couldn't
Who, then, would lead the latest years
Of Israel's battle's – but Yoav?

David: You are already old.

Yoav: I am still able — to fence with three young heroes!

David: It is depressing when a man must die
In irksome older age; but it is sadder, when
His time has passed, and he stubbornly persists.

(Enter Shlomo)

David: *(To Yoav)* I want to be alone with my son

Yoav: I haven't finished yet, I will be back. *(Exit)*

David: No one should even once comport himself
To me like you, my son, you conduct yourself
As is not befitting a son of the king.
You have amassed a throng of characters around
You — that call out for the devil.
That no one knows their home towns or their
Rearing, that frequent taverns, and is
Very prominent with derelicts and whores.

Shlomo: And with whom should I enjoy red wine
And pretty women – possibly, the elders?
Who knows if my strength will be enough?
And maybe if it is – if they will then befit me more.

David: I too, was young once,
And indulged in wine and pretty women
But besides women, there are also men:
Not only wine, there's also blood.
And there is not only a harp with music
But also a bow with arrows sharp.

Shlomo: By now I'll never be a warrior:
An elephant needs its trunk, a lion its claws
And sharp teeth, An ox needs horns
Same as a warrior must have
A sword, a spear, a bow and arrow.
A man, to shield himself in battle
Should have nothing but his brain and tongue.

David: And if it's hard for you to fight with swords
Then, learn to fight with a scepter
You have a lot of wisdom Shlomo,
Akhitofel too was very wise, and
Nevertheless, he ended like a fool.

Shlomo: Because in his life, he did not use his wisdom
But settled as a servant to the fool, Avshalom;
I do not need a sword, or scepter
Let Adoniyah's seek the crown for he's the eldest
But I – I only want the crown as a reward
For one's own song and wisdom.

David: You may be smart, but you lack something else:
Experience,
Wait too long and it could be
That your virtues will never be rewarded
Should Adoniyah seize the reigns,
He too, will be considered wise by the people.

Shlomo: Why should I want to rule the people?
All I need is a friend, a woman and a song.
Even a kingdom can rarely bring that much.

David: I have become unwell; I should go to my room and rest.
Consider it Shlomo, there isn't much time left, it could
Happen quickly. think!

(Exit David, Enter Yoav)

Yoav: The king's no longer here?

Shlomo: Not here.

Yoav: What did King David summon you here for?

Shlomo: Had my father wanted you to know,
He would not have let you go
And be alone with me.

Yoav: I sense from you like always, the smell of wine.
Don't you have any shame?

Shlomo: I sense from you like always, the smell of blood.
So tell me, who should be more ashamed?

Yoav: Your mother had taught you badly:
One doesn't frivolously get a crown.

Shlomo: My father had taught you badly:
One does not always become a leader of the army
Through murder!

Yoav: Your father was my partner.

Shlomo: My father killed only foreign enemies
But you, with your own hands, killed
Two great ministers from Israel.
And in addition, my father's not only
A warrior; he wrote wonderful songs.

Yoav: Long, long ago… when he was young
I heard that he wrote songs
Though I, I will confess to you – I can't…
But you can write songs too,
When I will come victorious from a battle
Then — you could praise and sing your songs
About my bravery.
You can also tenderly and prettily intone
The praises of Adoniyah the king.
For instance – to Avishag the Shunamit;

I imagine, that you will be doing this with joy
While to me it seems you should also make *her* happy

Shlomo: *(Pounces on him with clenched fists)*
Shut your mouth!

Yoav: *(Pulls out a sword)*
Careful boy!

(Shlomo steps back, Yoav leaves with a victorious mien,
(Enter Avishag)

Shlomo: How good, Avishag of you to come.
I see you and I am already cheerful.
Earlier I already had a conversation with Yoav
The army chief.
He is as rude and insolent as a common soldier.

Avishag: Watch out! You shouldn't quarrel with him, he is very strong!

Shlomo: And what does that word mean to me?
Nothing, not a thing!
Father had earlier summoned me to him and proposed that I should be his heir.

Avishag: *(Hugs and kisses him)*

My dear, my precious Shlomo!

Shlomo: Why does this, make you excited?
I made a point of declining him.

Avishag: That — I cannot understand. How could this be?

Shlomo: Understand this: I wish to remain free.

Avishag: Oh, how fitting would my black locks be to a golden crown!

Shlomo: But more beautifully will fit your black locks –
Some white flowers.

Avishag: If I came as a queen, to visit my birthplace of Shunam,
Every kith and kin will come out to meet me.
And all my friends explode with envy.

Shlomo: I do not envy the vain and foolish Adoniyah.

Avishag: Did you see Adoniyah when he conducts himself
In the loveliest streets in a chariot,
And fifty footmen run ahead
To honor him? – People open doors,
They open windows and they watch in wonder;
The young women stand on the roofs
And pelt him with the prettiest flowers
And spray him with the finest perfumes
How pretty, how gorgeous is he to behold!

Shlomo: Women open for me doors as well,
Without a chariot and fifty footmen.
They may not be pelting me with flowers
But throw themselves in my arms
And smell better than the finest perfumes.

Avishag: You are engaged enough with women, Shlomo,

Shlomo: I now see none but you: Avishag.

Avishag: Starting today, I could no more be summoned.

Shlomo: Why? What happened?

Avishag: Because of all people, Adoniyah should today become
The king of Israel

Shlomo: How does that prevent us from meeting?

Avishag: It is a hindrance; Adoniyah loves me and offered me…
To be his wife.

Shlomo: You will not agree. I want to hear you say that!

Avishag: You will such thing from me not hear.
I have an old cold king
And want from now, a young and hot one, he's here!
His name is Adoniyah!

(Exit Avishag)

Shlomo: Hear me out: I have decided: I regret it!
I want to be a king. I want, I must!
No one of you will know of my intelligence
While you are looking at it through the gates
Of the mighty – bent into submission.
I will bond my wisdom with my force and my resolve
Waging war with your respectability,
And you will tremble from it — terrified!
Yoav insulted me, and I jumped on him
With my clenched fists
So he pulled his sword and called me 'Boy',
Yes like a child I stood there, lost;
Powerless of shame and weakness
This will be no more. I will quickly see to it
Though, I don't know how. They don't know,
How strength along with wisdom –
Can be mighty, even deadly!

(Enter Batsheva)

Batsheva: Woe upon us, we are lost!

Shlomo: What happened? Answer!

Batsheva: Yoav and Evyatar the priest, have just now
Picked Adoniyah to be the king of Israel.

Shlomo: Not Adoniyah – *I* will be the king!

Batsheva: My son, what am I hearing?

Shlomo: I have so decided, and so it shall become!

Batsheva: *(Calls)*David! David!

(Enter David)

Shlomo: My father, and my King – bless me, empower me,
That I should become your true successor.
My crown will not be taken — away from my young head.

David: Be blessed my son, my heir.
I bequeath to you my crown and all my enemies,
Conduct yourself with wisdom so you keep the crown,
And free yourself from enemies.

(To Batsheva)

Batsheva, see, you have realized your dues,
I am rewarding you, for your pain and sacrifice!

(Both hug him. Enter Tsadok the priest, Nathan The prophet, Benayahu Ben-Yehoyadah, and other ministers)

David: You, my ministers, I am announcing to you that
I've earlier designated my son, Shlomo, as king!

All: Long live King Shlomo!

David: I cannot celebrate with you for I am ill
I give you in my name the prophet Nathan and
Tsadok the priest and also the minister Benayahu Ben-Yehoyadah –
In my name, they will anoint Shlomo.

(All leave)

How quiet of a sudden it has all become,
Not just around, but also it has deeply penetrated me.

(Sees the harp in the corner)

Ah, old harp, for years, like veins drained out of blood.
I see your strings now hanging ossified,
Forgive me for neglecting you,
For another bow.
A bow that has no more than one lone string
And plays with arrows, which brings
But tears, and rattle of bereavement.
The sounds have long fallen asleep
But if I will touch your strings
You will live again, with speech and song.

(Tries to play, behind him shows up Mikhal)

It's hard… so hard to make it work again…
I have from her extracted sound, now
From myself I should again extract the words
The words of just one song.
Ah God, how hard it is now to remember,
Who doesn't know my songs?
All sing them in the temple, in the streets,
Only I alone, the creator of the songs –
Do not remember them, forgot them all.

Mikhal: I was sitting with you in a small tent, and for me
It was the whole wide world.

David: Ah, what luck! I remember some!

(Repeats over)

I was sitting with you in a small tent, and for me
It was the whole wide world.

Mikhal: I sat with you by a quiet river and heard how
Both our hearts beat as one.

David: I sat with you by a quiet stream and heard
How both our hearts beat as one.

Mikhal: And even through the dark door of death
I will not fear while you are near.

David: How much comfort and peace in the lines.

(Repeats)

And even through the dark door of death
I will not fear while you are near.

(Quickly is heard a final sound, like a string snapping – It comes from David, Mikhal jumps quickly to him, and he falls dead in her arms)

Mikhal: I have brought back to your memory a song from your youth
That had captured the essence of your entire life.
You have lived with a sword with a spear and a bow
But from the song you have drawn and with a song you are gone.

(A sound of Shofar blowing is being heard. Enter Shlomo with the crown on his head. Nathan the prophet, Tsadok the priest, Benayahu Ben-Yehoyadah, soldiers, common people.)

A voice: Long live our new king Shlomo!

End

One Act plays from 'Last Writings'

The crying of a child

(Evening in a room. By the table sits a man of thirty six to seven years old. The doorbell rings. He goes to open it and soon comes back with another man)

Man: You need me?

Him: I beg your pardon; I came for the room to share in this dwelling.

Man: Yes, there is a free room here. It's the door on the left.

Him: And besides the room also there is?

Man: What do you mean?

Him: Whatever we may be sharing.

Man: Of course, of course, this is really a large dwelling. The kitchen and the bath also belong to you, and other superfluous things, of which my wife knows better. She'll be here soon. Please have a sit.

Him: Thank you. I have little time. I have to go get my things.

Man: Where do you keep your things?

Him: At the hotel, I've been staying there a few days.

Man: It is surely better in a private dwelling. In a hotel, a man feels himself constantly transitory.

Him: Knowing that this life is but transitory, is for me often a consolation. Getting used to the thought, that it's already so, and so it must remain — is too sad.

Man: You are by yourself?

Him: Like the majority — by myself.

Man: You have arrived here from the Soviet Union?

Him: Yes, and you?

Man: I was in the ghetto and in a camp. We are two separate people, ah?

Him: So it would seem. Whenever I happen to talk with people who were in a ghetto or camp, they think that I, having spent that time in the Soviet Union — will never properly understand them. Do you also think so?

Man: You consider yourself misunderstood? We the survivors, I really think that it's the opposite. We, for example, feel that you look at us with suspicion.

Him: Why do you think so?

Man: Well, because we remained alive. Why of all people, me?

Him: Nevertheless, not all think so. And those who look at you with suspicion… maybe do it out of resentment that among the survivors, there was none of their own? Yes, when at the end of the war we heard that such a small number of Jews remained alive, my acquaintances said: maybe by a chance there are among the survivors some of our close ones? I, however, did not have such illusions.

Man: This is not good for you.

Him: Those who believed it were really egotists. Six million Jews were killed and of all people just their relatives survived.

Man: Not egotists — hopeful.

Him: Call it what you like. And moreover — do you see the announcements in the newspapers? People are searching and searching. These are people who like to fool themselves.

Man: And I, being in a concentration camp, in very bad circumstances, I never stopped believing.

Him: And you found one of your own?

Man: No.

Him: You see…

Man: But I found a new close person — a woman.

Him: *(Looking at the crib in the corner)* and as I see — also a child…

Man: Yes, a woman and child.

Him: You will forgive me when I tell you that for me this is strange. After I heard and read about all the pain and humiliation that the Jews went through in the ghettos and camps; I thought that if it was possible for someone to save himself even from there, he is now — if not physically, then in any case, emotionally — not well. And here I see two people (she is probably also from a camp) and they got married and even have a child already.

Man: This is the life force of the living. The dead, as is the custom, do not walk in the street, but the living do. If the dead were walking around — It would not be possible to live.

Him: So according to you, we should forget the dead?

Man: The murder, we should not forget; but the murdered, we must learn to forget, if we want to go on living.

Him: I envy you. I too, would have liked to forget a lot, but unfortunately, I am not succeeding; are there many others like you? Here — your friends — and — I beg your pardon — your wife?

Man: There are some, like, among my friends, who think otherwise, and I try to pull them in that direction. And as pertains to my wife —

(*Thinks for some time*)

It is for her also, just hard to forget. It happens sometimes, — my name is Hirsh, and she calls me: David.

Him: David?! Is that the name of her husband?

Man: I do not know.

Him: And you do not ask?

Man: To what end? And possibly it really is the name of a brother of hers.

Him: (*Slowly, thinking, repeating mechanically*) and possibly it really is the name of a brother of hers. (S*omeone rings the doorbell*)

Man: Probably my wife. Excuse me for a minute!

(*He goes down. One can hear a short conversation from the other side of the door. She walks in. He gets up and walks toward her, suddenly they both cry out)*

Him: Esther!

She: David! (*She immediately takes control of herself)* Quiet! My husband should know nothing!

(*Her husband appears*. He *turns over to the wall like he would look at a picture* . She *stands by the table holding on to a chair*.)

Man: (*Holding her coat in his hand*) I wanted to hang it up, that coat of yours, but the hangar tore it up.

She: Put it away I will fix it soon.

Man: You look rather pale, what happened?

She: I… that is, with me… it almost happened…

Man: What almost happened?

She: Almost happened, an accident…

Man: You are upsetting me. What accident?

She: In the street… I was almost struck by a car…

Man: I did ask you not to go to the library now.

She: And I didn't even get a book. There were too many people, and I had to wait too long. I was afraid that the baby will meanwhile wake up while I was away.

(*She suddenly has an idea*)

would you possibly go there and get me a book?

(She caresses his face)

You are really not angry that I bother you…

Man: Good, I will.

(*Suddenly seeing Him, whom he completely forgot*)

Ah, Esther, this is our new neighbor. He lives here next door. (*Introduces them*) My wife and — he waits for him to say his name. (*He makes an incomprehensible sound.*) They usually wonder what else other than the room they are sharing. So they say. (*To him*) pardon me, I have to go. *(Leaves)*

(*They both remain motionless after his departure. He is the first to move away from his place, throws himself on her, hugs her, kisses her. She doesn't respond. In a moment, she frees herself from his arms and says to him, pointing at a chair*):

She: Sit down.

Him: Esther! (*He tries again to hug her*)

She: (*Harshly*) sit down!

Him: What is the matter with you?

She: You actually saw it; I have a husband.

Him: And I, what am I to you?

She: You *were* my husband.

Him: Just *were*? … Is he now for you more than me?

She: Yes, more. He is also the father of my child.

Him: With what right?

She: During the hardest years of my life, you were not with me. From the first day that you left, I felt abandoned.

Him: I went away because you wouldn't leave your family, your parents and your brothers.

She: Already, then, I was able to sacrifice for my family. You were not forced to do it.

Him: But can someone be blamed because he's away?

She: No.

Him: Moreover: could I have possibly imagined that the Germans will commit such horrors?

She: Also, possibly not.

Him: So what do you want from me?

She: The majority did well to be away, but when it comes to an individual, one should consider each case separately.

Him: And if you consider me separately?

She: It is for you much worse.

Him: Explain yourself!

She: It is hard to open old wounds, but it's lost. It's done. Listen: how old was I when you first met me?

Him: Twenty two.

She: And how many years did you lead me on until marriage?

Him: Strange, you should ask.

She: I have a reason. We carried on for six years. Why did you delay the marriage that long?

Him: Difficult economic conditions…

She: There are people who marry under worse material conditions. Additionally, however, to be able to do it, people have to believe in their own strength, in my strength. While after marriage we really, nevertheless, managed. And what happened later?

Him: Later?

She: I wanted to have a child. I told you that, and you mocked me and asked me, if it wasn't my mother who talked me into it, since she wanted a grandchild.

Him: And didn't I give you any other reason? Remember!

She: Yes. You also said, that now it is no time to have children that times are unsettled.

Him: I was correct now, wasn't I?

She: You were correct. But if trees should think that the wind could come and tear down their leaves — they would never bloom. You had a permanent fear of life and a fear of death, such that you were not capable of living or dying.

Him: And he… your husband… is better… better than me, ha?

She: I tested him during the very hard times which human imagination cannot even conceive. In the camp, where a piece of bread was a dream, he used to give me his share. He had a warm coat — and it was winter — he dressed me up in it. And as we came out of the camp, both of us had nobody, and he said to me: Esther, let's get married, let's build a new life. He said it so simply, that I could not refuse him. And just the same way I naturally bore him a child.

Him: And me, you totally forgot?

She: No, I remembered you. A few times I even tried to start a conversation about you with my husband, but he never showed any interest.

Him: But from now on — enough! You must be mine again.

She: This is now impossible.

Him: That really depends on you.

She: And if that happened?

Him: Than we shall both be happy.

She: Listen: four people stand in a circle. The first two — the two of us, and the other two, my husband and child. Do you hold it to be the truth that those who are the least guilty, that is: the father and child, should suffer, and us, who are the more guilty, ought to be, like you say — happy?

Him: The right thing is sometimes, as harsh as the wrong.

She: No, I will not deprive this child in the crib of his father, and forsake him. Because, for a second child — yours — I will not have milk in my breast, but poison.

Him: And this room could be my home. And you could be my wife, and this child — my child. Everything here I could have as the owner, and you take me for a stranger, an unwelcome guest.

She: And everything that you see here, you created? Now, when all is prepared, you would want to be the owner.

Him: Understand: I possibly have strength to bear the past, but I have absolutely no strength to start from the beginning.

She: I know, if I went back to you, what a pain this would be to tolerate you. You would torment me for years with questions about *him*, and would want to know every detail of our life together. You would, additionally, not live in the present, but with my past. Take him for example. You've only known him since last night. He came in, noticed that I was pale, but how easily I managed to divert his attention to something else. You would not have left me with a stranger. You would have been suspicious of everything.

Him: This is because I'm a simpler man.

She : That is not a deficiency. After the horrible events, I want to rest and live. Simply live. That does not mean, to just simply live without evaluating things. You, however, have a nature, of reaching conclusions before evaluating.

Him: And what should I do now?

She: Go away.

Him: Go to my place, to my room, and feel that so close…

She: By going away, I didn't mean from one room to another. Even if there were no wooden doors between us, but steel ones. You have to let go of this room, the city —

Him: This country, this world.

She: Don't turn this into rubbish.

Him: Must I really go away? My whole family and all my close ones have perished. Only one person remains alive — should I also deny myself of her? No! No!

(*He gets up hastily, throws himself at her, hugs her and kisses her*)

You are mine, mine!

(*From the crib is heard the crying of a child. She tears herself off his hands and leaps to the crib. He remains standing, helpless, looking with dejected stares at her*)

She: (*By the crib*) Sleep my child, my crown, ahh!

(*The child calms down*)

You shouldn't let a child cry.

Him: And a grown up, you could leave crying?

She: Grown-ups should know how to calm themselves.

(*Pause*)

Him: (*Slowly*) I have nothing left of you. Give me a picture, to remember you by.

She: Very well, I'll give it to you.

(*She goes to the closet, takes out a picture and hands it over to him*)

Him: Together with the child. Can't you give me a picture of you alone?

She: I, by myself, no longer exist. From now on, you should look at me only with a child.

Him: And will you say good bye to me?

(*She hugs him, kisses him, he pulls her to him and — tears himself away from her and runs quickly out of the room. She sits motionless for a while. Soon the doorbell rings, she shudders.*)

She: Did he change his mind?

(She goes to the door to open it and returns with her husband)

Man: I am back now. What is the matter? Have you been crying?

She: Suddenly I was feeling sad.

Man: I also suddenly felt sad on the way. I thought how good it would have been if one of our close ones lived here.

She: And it could possibly be sadder.

Man: What are you saying Esther? I don't understand you.

She: Well come here, come here, you are really so good. Let's kiss.

Man: Quiet down a bit. There is someone living next door.

She: No one lives there any longer.

Him: What are you saying? Didn't he just move in?

She: He'd already moved out.

Man: How strange. What could be the reason?

She: He would not live there, he's gone away from here, because…
Because there is a child here… because it will disturb him… that… crying of a child.

Only Ashes

(A room. an unlocking of the door from the outside is heard. Two men walk in)

He: Now here, as you see, that's where I live.

Friend: Wait a minute! This place looks familiar. Did you really live here before the war?

He: Yes it's the same dwelling.

Friend: (*Looking around*) As I see from the holly pictures on the wall, a Christian lives here too.

He: Also a Christian woman lives here.

Friend: She lives with you, or you live with her?

He: We live together.

Friend: Oh! This is interesting! I would have never imagined that you'd be living with a Christian woman.

He: And which of the past events that took place during the war you *did* imagine?

Friend: I thought that you'd told me everything on the way here.

He: We just met at the committee one hour ago. In one hour you want to know everything I went through during the years of horror?

Friend: Don't think I'm so naïve, I just thought that such an important thing, you would tell me first. How did you happen to get married?

He: She saved my life.

Friend: How did you find her?

He: Before the war she was our servant. When we were driven into the ghetto, she stayed in the house. After the uprising in the Warsaw Ghetto, I escaped in here. She received me well. Hid me real well in the dwelling.

Friend: You did, that is, hide in your own apartment?

He: Yes. This sounds strange. Imagine that: I was sitting here, locked up. Walking around the home where my parents and brothers lived. Every corner and every piece of furniture reminded me of them… their voices were still wandering around among the walls. The same grandfather-clock on the wall is now, like during my childhood, lulling me to sleep with its ticking and toking. But now I wasn't sleeping as calm and happy as before. Living here was in one respect better: I was not uprooted. But on the other hand, it was possibly more difficult for me to bear my loneliness, but enough about me! What do you plan to do next?

Friend: I first came here with a group of Jews from the Soviet Union. They are all going to lower Silesia. The train is coming in a few hours. I left my belongings with them and came down for a while to take a look at the Jewish Warsaw committee.

He: And you want to travel with these Jews to Lower Silesia.

Friend: Yes.

He: Would you possibly stay in Warsaw?

Friend: It is hard to find an apartment here.

He: Listen: here, over to the left, there is another room. You can live there. No one of my relatives and close ones is alive, I'd like to have you near.

Friend: Truth be told, you also are my only close one who remained alive. I also would like to be with you but…

He: No buts! Go to the train station and bring your things here.

Friend: I will go. Obviously, I will not burden you. As soon as I find another apartment, I'll move out.

He: That remains to be seen. Meanwhile, do your thing. The woman will probably come soon and prepare lunch. Go and do not tarry for too long.

(*The friend leaves, in a little while come up the wife and the mother in law*)

Wife: Well, well Marek, see who came here — mother!

He: (*To the mother*) you have become our frequent guest!

Mother: I think I'll be going back today.

Wife: Where are you running? Stay here for the night.

He: Yes… someone else will be spending the night here. A friend of mine; not only over night, but from now on, he will live in that room.

Mother: We have indeed met some stranger on the stairs. He appears to be a Jew. He probably came from *there.*

Wife: And why do we need to take in a sublet? Do we have such a large place? Or do you need some rent money?

He: Not for rental money, but simply: he is the only friend that remained alive.

Mother: It will be much healthier for you if you stopped altogether occupy yourself with Jews!

He: And why do *you* occupy yourself with a Jew?

Mother: *I* occupy myself with a Jew?

He: Yes. With me.

Mother: You are my daughter's husband, and — you are no longer a Jew!

He: I have become something new!

Wife: You still won't give up?

He: We will talk about it some other time. I'm going now to the attic. there should be in there a cot. My friend will sleep on it. (*leaves*)

Mother: You saw how he lit up, when I mentioned the Jews? You have to take full charge of him. You are too submissive. A wife…

Wife: Let it rest mama. You'll accomplish nothing with him.

Mother: Does he constantly befriend Jews?

Wife: From the very beginning. As soon as he came out of his hiding, he ran straight out looking for Jews. He used to disappear often. Once I followed him to the place he went. He went to their committee on Sheroka street.

Mother: This is not good, daughter. Why did you keep it away from me?

Wife: I always thought that this will end. But on the contrary, when the Jews began to come back from Russia, he became more emotional. Throughout the days he used to stay at the train station and wait for the trains. What draws you there? — I asked him, and he said: maybe I will find there a relative or a friend.

Mother: He already found a wife. What else is he looking for? He doesn't need more than that.

Wife: Each time I notice that some garment is missing from the closet. It turns out, that he's distributed them to the oncoming Jews.

Mother: Enough! Enough! I cannot hear it anymore! You really know, that when I and your father found out that you are hiding a Jew, how angry we were at you, but we suffered in silence. After that, it did not please us that you lived with him; but I thought to myself: he is quiet. He doesn't drink; he doesn't beat you — let it be. Maybe in time he'll become one of us; but this which you are now telling me, is not happy! It shows that the devil is pulling him back. This little bird can one fine day, fly away!

Wife: And what should I do with him?

Mother: Let us not be so desperate! If he did not exist, there will be someone else who wanted you.

Wife: Mama, don't talk of it!

Mother: I already see that you really love him. That of all people, you want him, a Jew. That I will not that easily remove him from your head. But you should not let him go further! I have an idea.

Wife: What kind of idea?

Mother: Let's you and him move in with me.

Wife: He will not want to.

Mother: Being his wife, you have to influence him. A wife needs to know all the weaknesses of her husband and know how to use them for her own advantage when she needs to.

Wife: And how will I be safer with him over there?

Mother: Over there, there are no Jews at all. There will be no one to remind him and awake in him his Jewishness.

Wife: And if he'll insist and not want to go?

Mother: He must go! He must! And… wait. I have an idea: tell him that you're pregnant. One can never know for sure, whether his wife is pregnant or not. You will tell him, that you want to have that child at my place, so that I can help you from the start. He will have to come here too, and in barely a short time I will do all — he will not go away from there. Do you understand me?

Wife: I see that you fuss a lot over him. It will really be good if we all lived together. You will help me to better hold him in my hands.

Mother: What do you know, a mother has a purpose! I wish you had turned to me from the very beginning! We would not have come to all this trouble. Can you be trusted to do it all like you should?

Wife: I'll try my best.

Mother: I'd like you to go with me right away, and that said guest of yours leave. Listen, I'll go now to the second room. He will probably come back soon. Tell him, that I suddenly don't feel good and must lie down. That is, so that you can convince him. If I hear that you need my help, or that he's persuading you — I'll be standing behind the door and listen to your talk, and come in.

(*Exit mother*)

(*He comes up. Busies himself with pulling out the bed*)

He: My friend didn't come yet?

Wife: No. And about mother you don't ask anything?

He: Then where is she?

Wife: In the second room. She all of a sudden got a headache so she lay down, I've been so worried!

He: Well, sure.

Wife: What's sure?

He: Sure you'd be worried, it's your mother.

Wife: And you're not concerned with her?
If you only knew how she thinks about you!

He: Maybe all that thinking about me gives her a headache, ah?

Wife: You always talk about her like that; she feels it and gets upset.

He: Let her interfere less with our lives and she'll be less upset.

Wife: She only means well for us. (*Comes closer to him*)
She's all by herself; all alone in her old age.

Him: She's not alone there. She has her neighbors, the same church, the market.

Wife: You think ill of her. She loves us. The father is no longer alive. She would want us to live close to her. She really talked to me about it today.

Him: Does that mean that she wants to increase her living inventory?

Wife: She wants nothing for herself. She wants, that we take over the house and all of the house-keeping.

Him: Before the war, your father was just a barber. How come all of a sudden he became a merchant? How did he get a house and a store? I know. The house is from a Jew, and the possessions — from Jewish things. No. I am not drawn to that house, with that household!

Wife: But I must go there.

Him: "Must?" Why must you?

Wife: Because… because I'm pregnant. I want to be with mother. By myself I won't be able to manage.

Him: What did you say? You are pregnant? But this is not possible!

Wife: Why couldn't it be? I am not sick now, am I?

Him: I mean, I've been careful.

Wife: One can never be sure.

Him: If this is the case — you must abort that child!

Wife: You really do not want to ever be a father? I often see how you play with the neighbor's child. You are so good to him, it simply becomes you. This is a stranger's child — imagine how much you would love your own!

Him: No. I will not have my own child!

Wife: Why not?

Him: Because of what will our child be, A Jew or a Christian?

Wife: Obviously, a Christian.

Him: And why shouldn't he be a Jew like his father?

Wife: As if you didn't suffer enough from your Jewishness, now you want to bequeath it to your son?

Him: I'd rather give my child the hard bequest of my father, which cost his life and that of millions more, than the bequest of your father, that came from their death. I'm telling you once more: the child's upbringing will further deepen the divide between us.

Wife: And to me it seems that you talk a lot about your people because you don't love me. If you did love me, you would have sacrificed everything for my sake.

Him: You never *did* ask me if I loved you, now, did you?

Wife: True, I never did. I was afraid to… In any case, I believed that you will live with me, get used to me and come to love me. And now — enough playing. You have nothing to fear. I'm not pregnant. I was only testing you. But regardless of that, I think that we ought to be with mother.

Him: I will not go there.

Wife: You will not yield anything to me, nothing. You are so insistent over every little thing! If it weren't for me, you will now be lying under the rubble of the ghetto!

Him: It is easier to die and end it all than to be a living dead.

Wife: I am a plain woman and don't understand your talk. I only know how much toil and pain it cost me to hide you. My mom and dad warned me of the great danger, that I was in, but I answered them: I love him and what will happen to him — let it happen to me.
Without him I cannot live anyway! How many nights I cried in my sleep, while dreaming that the Gestapo discovered your hiding place and came to take you away. With each suspicious rustle, with every knock on

the door, I used to tremble along with you. You are already forgetting all that?

Him: I haven't forgotten that. I will be forever grateful to you; but gratefulness alone is still too little to hold together a husband and wife. You say you love me. What is it in me that you love?
All that I consider to be my very being — is alien to you.

Wife: You are, surly, more educated than I am. You understand a lot of things in the world more than I do, but nevertheless there were times when I proved stronger than you. Remember, when you had enough of lying hidden and you told me, that you will turn yourself in to the Germans? Remember, how much trouble it was for me to convince you, to prevent you from doing it. I often used to invent good news from the front, though there weren't always any, to make you strong, and encourage you to remain in hiding.

Him: This is all true. I always admired your strong faith in life.

Wife: And from where do you think I got so much strength? — From my love for you.
(*She comes closer to him*)
I feel that you are thinking of leaving me. Where will you go? Who in the world do you have? You will go looking for a new unknown friend, when In that very same time you already have a proven one. You once had a mother, a father, and brothers; they no longer live. It is possible that no one you knew in this world, is alive, except the two of us.

Him: (*Broken up*) what do you want from me? Say it.

Wife: You should be with me. You should follow me and go to my mother. (*He is silent*) Well, will you go?

Him: I will go.

Wife: (*Kisses him*) this is how I like you!
(*She opens the door and the mother comes in*)

Mother: I already feel better my children. I will be going home.

Wife: Mama, I'd just had a talk with Marek. He agrees that we should move to Louyvitch.

Mother: This is good! I think that you should do it right away. You should sell the dwelling. Indeed, I have a buyer. He's marrying off a daughter of his, and this young couple has no place to live. Let's go to him now.

Him: So fast? What's the hurry?

Mother: I would like to empty it before going home.

Wife: Can we first eat something?

Mother: (*Gives her a nudge and says quietly*) don't interfere!
(*To him*)
You're coming with me?

Him: No. I cannot go. I'm waiting for a friend.

Mother: I will not go all by myself. One of you must come with me. (*To her daughter*) Could you go with me?

Wife: So be it. (*To husband*) Watch over the kitchen. That late, and we still haven't had lunch. A rattled day! Make sure the fire doesn't go out.

(*The mother and daughter go down. After some time, enters the friend*)

Friend: I'm back. Brought with me all of my so called belongings. Once, Jews used to wander from one country to another with a sack. Now we became modern — we have suitcases.

Him: (*Sits Motionless staring at one point*)
During the time that you went away,
the situation has changed.

Friend: In what way?

Him: I'm going away.

Friend: I don't understand you, first you convinced me not to go — and now…

Him: I'm not going to lower Silesia, I'm going to Louyvitch. My wife and mother in law were here. It was at the point that I should go totally away from them, but now it turns out , that I should go — away from you.

Friend: And why did you do it?

Him: Because she saved my life.

Friend: Did she save you because, she just wanted to help a Jew, out of kindness, or she wanted to save you for herself?

Him: She probably has her own intentions. But does it change the fact that she put her life on the line for me? I, too, should sacrifice mine!

Friend: One individual cannot demand from another that he should sacrifice his life for him. This right is only a norm of the community at large.

Him: The community at large — I'm already tired of carrying the pain of the community! I want once and for all, to be free of the troubles and torments of generations!

Friend: If so — there is nothing else for me to do. I'm leaving.

Him: Where will you go?

Friend: Back to my friends.

Him: Don't go away. Stay in the apartment.

Friend: If I decide to stay, it is only to be with you. If you're going away. Why would I remain here in the apartment?

Him: You won't stay?

Friend: I don't understand at all why you'd want me to stay.

Him: For what? You see… If you remain here, I still have the ability, at last, to come back…

Friend: And I think that you have to make a firm decision. That attitude is not healthy for you, or for her.

Him: I already promised that I would go… so I will go… I'm going to Louyvitch… I will live among burghers, run her

father's business, chase hay, buy foreign currency and wait for 'better days' ah?
On Sundays I will dress up and go to church with my wife. And when a Christian holiday comes, I will walk in the procession through the streets with icons and crosses. The bells will ring: bom-bom-bom!...

(Jumps up and cries:)

No, No! This will not be! Save me from them! Don't let me go there!

Friend: What happened to you all of a sudden? You are pale! You are trembling all over!

Him: I remember, how as a child, when a procession used to pass through our street. Mother used to carry me into the house. She used to be pale and whisper a prayer that they would go through and won't bother anyone. Not invent a blood libel. Once there was a procession going through in our street. I was standing on the balcony and playing. When the procession went by our house, bent over in the balcony, to better see, and my yarmulke fell into the middle of the procession! There was a great commotion below. There were outcries against Jews. Rocks were thrown into windows. The mob tore into Jewish houses.

Mother grabbed me and found a safe place for me behind the closet. I heard yelling, crying, a clattering from windows. At eight years of age, already feeling the taste of Jewishness. Hear, hear me out: this is the same closet behind which I hid over twenty years ago!

(*He's finished. There is a moment of silence*)

Friend: I will go. I do not want to be late. I will go with my friends.

Him: I'm coming with you!

Friend: Is this your final decision?

Him: Yes we're going together!

Friend: If so, pack your things quickly.

Him: No, no! I will take nothing with me. Nothing! But I will write a few words.

(*Writes a note, Leaves it on the table*)

Friend: We're off

(*both exit. After a little time come in the wife and Mother*)

Mother: Why is it dark in here?

Wife: Where did he disappear?

(*Lights a light*)

Mother: I'm very hungry we should prepare some food, (*Goes to the kitchen*)

Wife: (*Sees the note*)

What is that? Who wrote it? (*reads*) Oh, Jesus!

Mother: (*In the kitchen*)

men come and men go. Here all is burned, only ashes remain, only ashes…

End

After the deluge

(*In the ark, various animals are strolling and engaged in conversation*)

Wolf: (*To lamb*) I do not understand, and I cannot conceive, how I once could have been so cruel. Each time when I saw you I used to be wild and full of murder. Remembering that, I must bow my head in shame, and my lips stammer: please forgive me!

Lamb: Your voice, uncle, which used to scare me so — is now ringing in my ears, like the sweetest melody from a shepherd's fife. But in my heart I always thought that you are not driven to murder from evil but from hunger.

Wolf: And hunger, you think, justifies everything! Why do I need your flesh, when so much grass and so many herbs grow out of the earth? Their aroma is more pleasing than your blood! I am raising my front paw and swear an oath: as soon as I get out of the ark, I am going to a doctor that he should pull out all my teeth and to a barber — that he should clip my claws down to my flesh.

Hawk: (*To the dove*) Lovey-dovey of mine, everyone knows that I have a sharp eye, but now I am seeing you for the first time: many things I haven't seen! Even in the very strangest dream: that I would see myself go with you on a stroll, and speak so tenderly about love and happiness? I would think of descending upon you straight away and devouring you.

Dove: Wouldn't you, dear, God forbid, die of hunger?

Hawk: Recently you cooked for me some mushrooms and they taste better than flesh. Even the tongues of your sister didn't taste so good to me!

Dove: Nevertheless, I will tell you the truth: your pointy beak still scares me a little.

Hawk: If that's important to you, I will not hesitate for a minute. I will try to grind it against the rocks, or better yet — I will deep it over-night in salt water. You will see, it will become as soft as a cooked carrot.

Dove: And another thing, listen: if you want to be refined and respectable, then quit your vagrant life of abandon over forest and mountain.

Hawk: You are correct. I shall forego both forest and mountain; sit under a human roof and along with you, morning and evening coo about the fortunes of amicable homeliness.

Dove: And It's been so many days now, that Noah had sent my husband to find out about the deluge, and he still tarries, and he's not coming back.

Hawk: He has certainly left you and betrayed you. Forget the unfaithful, false husband! I've been dreaming for so long of a quiet, gentle wife such as you.

Dove: (*curious*) And *your* wife?

Hawk: My wife is mean, she's tough — she's manly!

Dove: And I, for a long while, have been dreaming of you. I used to be terrified of you, but equally looked to you with delight.

Hawk: And your husband?

Dove: My husband is weak and pale — a woman.

(*The conversation between them is quiet and sad*)

Spider: (*To the fly*) I am an artist. I weave my threads over corners and cracks and bond them. But now, I do confess my sin: I have converted my art into a net for trapping those who are weaker than myself. I've used the art only for the stomach. Ach, how regretful and pained I feel because of it!

Fly: Are you possibly thinking of tearing your threads that tie you to your sinful past?

Spider: That would not be a small crime like the previous one. Talent is a blessed gift from God! It ought to be utilized for the good of the creatures and to ennoble and purify their virtues.

Fly: Then what do you think of weaving now?

Spider: I shall weave nets for womanly countenances, and in the nets, I will not catch, innocent flies, but sinful manly stares, so that they may not weaken chastity and modesty!

Snake: (*To the woman*) Oh, beautiful wondrous woman! men have spread many lies about us. They wanted to separate us from the very beginning.

Woman: Do not apologize, it is not necessary. No one will separate the woman from the snake.

Snake: I hear a fiddle playing, I raise my head, I listen and I'm touched, enchanted and not only by the music, I also love beauty, and if I love beauty, how could I hate you?

Woman: I love you too. I always love those who lie at my feet…

Snake: And while I lie at your feet, it is possible all the more to wonder at your pretty feet…

Woman: God had once changed your appearance, but not your brain. You still speak beautifully and seductively as you used to.

Snake: I speak to you so well, because it often seems to me that God did not make you from Adam's rib, but from mine...

Woman: And if you speak the truth and look for my welfare, I have a great request from you: we are soon going out to a new world, and indeed, possibly, also to a new paradise. Give me no more an apple from the tree of knowledge but from the tree of life, I want to live forever!

Snake: Why live forever? Beauty lasts even a shorter time than your short life.

Woman: No, no! Not only do I want to live forever, but I also want to be young and pretty forever!

(*Enter Noah*)

Noah: (*To the wolf*) Wolf! Howl three times — a sign for everyone in the ark to come together.

(*The wolf takes to howling. Enter Noah's entire family, all the animals, birds and frogs.*)

Noah: Didn't anything new happen with you? Doesn't anyone have any complaints about someone else?

(*All quiet*)

Did I possibly mistreat any of you? If there is such someone here, let him come up and speak openly!

Voices: No such thing!
— Who's talking about mistreatment?
— You helped us!
— Saved us from death!
— Long live grandpa Noah!
— Long live!

Noah: If so — we shall part in peace.

Voice: We do not want to part with you; we want to spend with you many more days.

Noah: No my dears. The dove hasn't returned. This is a sign that out there it is better. The end of the journey, prepare yourself to get out!

(*no one moves*)

Why are you standing there sad and worried? After the crowding and darkness in the ark, when in front of you a world awaits, greater and full of light?

Voice: And what shall we eat there in your world?

Noah: In the ark I cared for you, in the free world — you are in God's care.

Voice: We want to eat!
— We want bread!
— We want meat!

Noah: Where will I get that? The stores are empty.

Voice: He's hiding all the food!

Parrot: (*Repeating*) He's hiding all the food!

Voice: He ate all the meat, and I, the bones!

Parrot: He ate all the meat, and I, the bones!

Voice: He fed us with worm infested peas!

Parrot: He fed us with…

Voice: With stale flour!

Parrot: With stale…

Bear: And he ordered me to chop wood!

Beaver: And me — to peel potatoes and sweat!

Squirrel: And me — to grind horseradish and cry!

Voice: Let's eat him!
— His wife!
— His sons!
— His sons' wives! …

Shem: What is he to us? Exactly like everyone else, we only are invited guests

Kham: (*Pointing at Noah*) He whom you previously praised — now you chastise!

Yeffet: We have no part in his affairs.

Daughter in law : We should have gotten rid of him long ago.

(*The sons and daughters in law separate from Noah The animal circle around Noah becomes tighter.)*

Noah: A moment ago, when you thought that you will remain longer in the ark, and will need to receive my favor — you thanked me, you flattered and praised me; but now when you hear that there is no more a deluge — you want to eat me. Well, good, I agree. But my thin body will not satisfy all of you —

Voice: Not all, *I* will eat you!

Voice: Why you? — Me!

Voices: Me! … Me! ... Me! ...

Noah: I already see that you cannot come to an agreement. None of you will give up my body for another.

Parrot: I!...

Voice: Nothing left to do. Come on let's go!

Noah: Maybe God had prepared for you plenty of food

outside.

Animals: Come, let's go! Faster! Quicker!

(*All the animals push and try to get out first, they yell, they fight, they forget Noah entirely.*)

Lion: Make room!

Fly: (Jumps up on top of the lion) Make way, make room for us!

Elephant: (*waves his trunk left and right*) Step aside, Step aside!

(*The lion and the elephant exit. By the door various animals Bicker, each wants to get out first*)

Lamb: (*To wolf*) Help me get out uncle.

Wolf: Away! While you still have your hooves.

Dove: (*To hawk*) Carry me with you my dear!

Hawk: Such as you, I only carry in my stomach!

Dove: Ah, you hypocrite (*weeps*) my husband, my faithful husband!

Fly: (*to the spider*) tie me to you with a thread and take me with you.

Spider: Don't buzz in my ear!

(*The congestion increases, the yelling — louder. All fight and trample one another until the ark is slowly emptied. In a corner some of Noah's household members, are consulting with each other over what to do next. Soon comes running from the other side, the lamb soaked with blood, the eyes filled with anguish. It shakes with its entire body and clings to Noah.*)

Lamb: Grandpa Noah, Grandpa Noah! Protect me from the wolf!

(*The dove falters in, the white feathers bloodied. She falls powerless at Noah's feet*)

Dove: The hawk, Oy, the hawk!

Noah: What happened?

Dove: Hacked me with his beak… with his talons… Oy I'm fainting… I'm falling… I'm dying…

(*The crying from all directions gets louder. Noah opens wide the door — in front of the door there's a puddle of blood.)*

Noah: God! You have drained out the deluge of water, but apparently the deluge of blood will forever seethe upon your land!
Was it worth it to annihilate so many humans and animals so that on the first day of the second genesis the earth will again be filled with predation and murder?!

(*From a corner Noah is approached by his three sons and daughters in law*)

Shem's Wife: The animals are all out, we are alone. What do we do now?

Noah: We do the same as they: we get out of the ark.

Yeffet's Wife: Look how he's pushing us around! We are the same ark owners as he is!

Noah: Since when do you like the ark so much, dear daughter in law?
— recall how, when I was building the ark, how you used to say that I'd lost my mind; that I was senile, that my head was seized by madness. I carried the boards all by myself, cut and planed them and smeared them with pitch. You didn't let any of my sons come and help me. But when the deluge broke out, you all came running to me, fell at my feet begging: dear father in law save us, let us in — give us a small place in your ark!

Shem's Wife: What should you have done? Ah? Not let in your own flesh and blood?

Noah: And as I let you in, I became smaller: you began to carry into the ark the beds, the closets, the mirrors, the tables. You wanted to carry in everything with you; even the washtub, the grater, and the mortar and pestle. It really seems like you have more things now than you had in your own houses. Apparently you nudged it away from the neighbors.

Yeffet's Wife: Another father in law, would have enjoyed his sons having such enterprising wives, and he — is still complaining.

Shem's Wife: Now we are going out into the world. How shall we make a living? Give us dear father in law, the keys of the store room.

Noah: I can give you the keys, but what will you get out of it? In the storeroom nothing remains.

Yeffet's Wife: What? You gave it all to the animals?! They were more loyal than us?!

Noah: God put them in my custody. I had to take care of them.

Shem's Wife: So give us the gold and diamonds.

Noah: From where should I all of a sudden have gold and diamonds? I am a poor Jew.

Yeffet's Wife: And you didn't hide anyone? You didn't smuggle in anyone on board, and were paid for it with gold and diamonds?

Noah: How can you say that? Remember: people came knocking on the ark, crying, sobbing, begging to get in. I used to crawl into the farthest corner, so that I won't hear the crying and weeping of the old, the women and children. But you jostled to the window, wanted to see, how the people and animals were carried and torn away by the frothing currents, how they tussled, choked breathlessly, and floated around, dead and swollen.

Shem's Wife: But what does that have to do with the matter?

Noah: Wait a minute. I once saw through the window, how our neighbor Raize-Gittel, runs with a child in her hand, in a kishele, beating her chest crying and begging; you can leave me out but take my child in. I was dumbfounded, forgot everything and ran to open the door for her, but you jumped at me blocked my way and yelled: you want to let strangers in the ark? You want to break God's command? That was the first time I heard you mentioning God's name.

Yeffet's Wife: but the neighbor was a poor widow! You are not obliged to do it for free!

Shem's Wife: What's the use of complaining! Father in law, stop playing innocent, and get out the food and money!

Noah: Here are the keys, go and see for yourself if there is anything in the storeroom and take it. Come see me if you find a penny.

Shem's Wife: (*Smacks her hands*) Well, how can you fix such a disaster? He really is a saint!

Yeffet's Wife: naïve!

Shem's Wife: If I had known that your father was a pauper I would have forbidden him from going into the ark. Never mind, I already knew that you were a schlimazel but I thought that you, the eldest son, will receive the larger part of your father's inheritance. And here it appears that he is such a pauper and such a schlimazel, like you! I can no more believe what I see with my own eyes!

Shem: Good, I wanted to leave anyway.

Shem's Wife: What's he saying? Where is he going?

Shem: I've been devout; I used to sit throughout the days till late at night and study. I heard it said that life offers many pleasures — but I didn't want to taste them, because each pleasure is bound with sin. I made peace with the harsh punishment that God gave the old world, because I believed that the new world will be a better one. But the new world is not better. Is creation guilty again, or indeed, possibly the creator?

Shem's Wife: Woe is me, it sounds like he's speaking against God!

Shem: If the creator is to blame, I'll go to him and make him account for all the dead!

Shem's Wife: He's lost his mind! How will you go to God? How will you find him? He really is up there in heaven!

Shem: I will build a tower all the way up to heaven! I will go up to him and then: let him give me an answer.

Shem's Wife: And leave me here alone?

Shem: I don't want to know from family, or from my own happiness, unless I get an answer from God.(*Exit*)

Shem's Wife: (*chasing after him*) Thief, assassin! How do you have the heart to leave me here all alone, an abandoned wife! (*Exit*)

Yeffet: (*To wife*) Why are you still here dear? Come on out! Under the happy sky. Here it is dark, here the air is suffocating I want to breath freely.

Yeffet's Wife: And where shall we live?

Yeffet: The old house is destroyed — we shall build a new one. A white house with red shingles on the roof. With wild vines over the windows, and a flower garden in front of the house.

Yeffet's Wife: And how are we going to make a living?

Yeffet: We'll go to the forest and pick berries. Drink fresh water from a spring.

Yeffet's Wife: And where will I get dresses?

Yeffet: It really is a new genesis. Think of it as though I am Adam and you are Eve. Why dresses? A fig leaf is enough!

Yeffet's Wife: Where will I —

Yeffet: (*Interrupts her*) Oh, ask no more! Nature is bountiful, she will give us everything. She is waiting for us. Come my dear, my beloved, come!

(*He grabs her by the hand and pulls her out*)

Noah: And you Kham, where will you go?

Kham: I will remain here.

Noah: (*Dumbfounded*) What?!

Kham: Yes, father. I want to stay with you.

Noah: What are you saying? Shem is away, Yeffet is away, and you of all people, want to stay with the old father?

Kham: Why are you so surprised?

Noah: I know… you haven't been my… most successful son.

As a child you used to fight with the neighbors' children. Every time, came another neighbor, whose window you broke or orchard you ripped, and later… later you used to bother all the servants and the cooks. And you of all people want to be the supporter of your father in his old age?

Kham: Yes father. Once I was very sinful. But after the deluge I've changed entirely. I am now pious and good.

Noah: I thank you Lord of the universe, for your great favor! I was blasphemous, thinking that the deluge did not improve anyone. But my son Kham did learn something from it. Today it is for me a holiday. A holiday!

Kham: Of course today is a holiday. A double holiday: the water has subsided and I became pious and good. Can we possibly have a meal in honor of it?

Noah: Surely we ought to, my son. I still have somewhere bread, a herring and some cheese.

Kham: That is fine, but how do we celebrate without drinking?

Noah: Right, we should have a drink Khamenyoo. The doctor forbade me from drinking. It damages my kidneys, but never mind, today I must drink!

(*He brings out bread, herring, cheese and several bottles of wine*)

Let us sample a little.

(*Noah pours two glasses of wine*)

Kham: Cheers, Papa!

Noah: Cheers! (*both drink, he coughs*) Oy it's strong, it's strong! It takes away my breath!

Kham: Eat something, papa, this is because, you haven't been drinking for so long (*pours a second glass*) the next one will be better.
Cheers!

Noah: (*Drinks*) A good bit of drink!

Kham: And here comes a third glass. So many days and weeks with only water around us, and more water, now this water is flowing —
Cheers!

(*They drink the third glass*)

Noah: (*Stands up tottering drunkenly*) Kham… Khamenyoo… come here, let me give you a kiss…

Kham: (*To himself*) we can now begin. (*loud*) papa you know. We have to think about real things, about making a living. From what will you, that is, we are going to live?

Noah: I'll be… I'll be a caretaker in a temple…

Kham: Why of all things a caretaker?

Noah: A holy place… Torah… and on every death anniversary… I could get a drink…

Kham: (*To himself*) He's got some logic (*loud*) why of all thing a caretaker? Why serve others? One should be his own boss. Here, be an owner of the ark. It is not really some plain box but the ark, Noah's ark! A world went under with people and animals, but the ark has survived! It is the only thing, left over from the old world. The only memory. It should be turned into a museum.

Noah: Khamenyoo… you really never wanted to learn… Not reading books… Where do you get this inte… intelligent talk?

Kham: True, I don't like to read books, but in return, I used to go to read newspapers and go to rallies. Yes, so what do I think? — With a museum, people will come into the ark. We cannot charge a high price, but there's no harm. The greater hall on the other side of the ark we'll rent for weddings.

Noah: For poor brides, orphans…

Kham: Why only for orphans, and other Jewish daughters need to wait? Let there be more Jewish weddings, let Jews increase and multiply! And when there are no wedding, we will rent the hall for an evening-dance.

Noah: A what? Evening dance?

Kham: Let Jews be happy, Let Jews dance!

Noah: (R*epeating*) Let Jews be happy… let Jews dance… — A good thing!

Kham: It will pay off, papa. It will enrich the people. (*He pours out two more glasses*) To the success of the new undertaking. (*They both drink*) You see papa, on the left side we shall have the museum. The museum with the holy artifacts commemorating the lost world. On the other side, on the right — the dance hall with the small rooms underneath. If you want to be solemn and cry — Left, please! But in case it's the opposite, and you want to enjoy yourselves and wile away the time — to the right please! Why are you sitting looking at me with glazed eyes? Here, have another drink!

Noah: (*Drinks, stammers*) — I want — Left! … I want — ha-hee- hee- hee-hee!

(*He starts to tear off his clothes and sing*):

If God wanted animal and men
To harshly reprimand,
Why did he really miss
Punishing the fish?
For them a deluge is
A finer thing indeed
When everybody's drowned
They only swim around
Rise quickly to the top
Eat everybody up.
A world is dead, upset,
But, their numbers swell
Is it good like that?
Oy ram tsu ri ri rah!
And where is justice, ha?
Ha hopsa hopsa sa!

(*Kham opens the door wide. Stands by the threshold and cries out into the street*)

Kham: Estimable public! We have opened in the ark a museum dedicated to the memory of the millions who perished in the deluge. You will see here fragments of dead people and skeletons of women and children. You will see here photographs of the people, when the deluge rushed in. how they ran in horror, how they screamed, wanted to hold on to the ark, that they saw before their eyes. But the waves tore them away and they drowned.

Come and see the said pictures that will shock you, that will freeze the blood in your veins! Among the victims you will surely be able to find your relatives and friends!

And here to the right — Very estimable guests! Here on the right, we opened a bar. We have furnished the bar according to the latest fashion. With mirrors, with neon lights, with the best orchestra, with various drinks and with the most charming women!… As the first night attraction, will be presented the saintly man, the virtuous, grandpa Noah. We have succeeded in recruiting him to our enterprise. Behold, observe him, there he stands half naked and dancing! Tickets please! There are still a few tickets left!

(*Enter Shem and Yeffet with their wives*)

Yeffet: We've heard something outlandish, what's going on here Kham?

Kham: Very simple: I opened in the ark, a museum and a bar.

Shem: And what is papa doing there, drunk?

Kham: He's performing for me at the bar.

Yeffet's wife: You see Yeffet, when you were looking for cobwebs and spices, your brother has been making a good living.

Shem's Wife: Nah, look Schlimazel, when you were crawling into heaven, Kham had captured the earth!

Shem: No! I will not let him make a living from misfortune! Papa get out of there!

Kham: Don't take him! I have a part in him too!

Yeffet: No! No! You don't have a right to him!

Kham: Shush, Shush! Don't think you will upstage me, take away the bargain! I will right away engage a comedian he will play for me the role of the saintly Noah. He will play it better than the real one. The real one always plays badly.

(*He turns to the public in the street*)

Estimable crowd! Due to technical reasons we are closing the show tonight. We are selling tickets for tomorrow!

(*From all sides, people are coming to the ticket booth*)

End

In the bunker

(*In the bunker. it is dark; suddenly it becomes more illuminated. The light is coming from an opening above. Through the opening slides himself in, another man. He doesn't have time to look around, when through the opening comes another one.*)

Wolf: Who is that?

Hershel: Another Jew.

Wolf: You saw me getting in?

Hershel: Yes.

Wolf: And no one else?

Hershel: No one else. (*coughing*) What a smell! I'm choking. What is it?

Wolf: That means that the Germans have discovered the bunker, and let in the gas. I must enlarge the opening, to let the gas out. (*He does that, more light gets in.*)

Hershel: (*Cries out*) Human bodies on the ground!

Wolf: Probably gassed.

Hershel: It's horrible!

Wolf: The bodies have been stiff for a while.

Hershel: But look, the bunker leads to a sewer!

Wolf: I had known of it earlier, and that's why I came here.

Hershel: Could we save ourselves?

Wolf: This we shall see. Meanwhile we ought to rest and gather our strength. Plenty of bedding here — we'll rest a little. (D*oes that*) so many sleepless nights! And you, what are you standing there for, gaping? Lie down. You're such a hero, ah?

(*Hershel lies down near him*)

How did you manage to pull through till now? Thousands of people have died of hunger and you survived? Hundreds of thousands of nice and healthy people sent to the ovens, — and such as this remains!

Hershel: My brother, my brother Leib helped me. I've been sickly since I was a child. He never let any harm come to me. I was four years old when my father died so he became my father. He'd saved me twice from the Umschlagplatz*

Wolf: And what was he? A policeman?

Hershel: No. But he's strong, much stronger than you. And brave there's no one like him!

Wolf: And where is he now?

Hershel: I do not know. He's one of those who participated in the uprising. He went out once to fight, and left me in the bunker.

---

* A city square in Warsaw, used as a transfer point to the death camps

Meanwhile the house was on fire and I escaped in here.

(*A noise is heard. Hershel springs to his feet in fear*)

Did you hear?

Wolf: There is nothing to be afraid of — it's the rats, they have plenty of dead to eat.

(*Hershel stands up. Looks for something*)

Wolf: Why did you get up? What are you looking for?

Hershel: I'm looking for something to throw at them.

Wolf: You are a fool. It won't help.

Hershel: We shall see.

(*Throws something in the direction of the noise. It turns quiet.*)

You see, it became quiet!

Wolf: What did you do it for?

Hershel: Let the rats not eat people.

(*The noise from the rats is heard again*)

Wolf: Here they're back.

Hershel: I will chase them away!

Wolf: They will chase *you* away! They are bold and can even assault the living. Better hear me out; we will soon go through the sewer. Possibly we'll manage to save ourselves through the Arian side. In such rags you may not show yourself above ground, you must get some other clothes.

Hershel: How would I get other clothes in the bunker?

Wolf: Can't you figure out anything? Here lie around the dead, right? Pull the clothes off someone. And look in everybody's pockets and on their wrists they may carry a watch — all of that will be useful to us here.

Hershel: I will not rob the dead!

Wolf: And that the rats will eat them with their clothes is better? Do you know how many times I saw the living pull off the clothes off the dead?

Hershel: I won't do it.

Wolf: The way you put it, your brother helped you. Did *he* undress the dead for your sake?

Hershel: You shouldn't say anything bad about my brother! You hear! Because…

Wolf: (*Grabs him and flings him to the ground*)

Because what? I gave you a strong suggestion, and will not tolerate such chicken talk! I'm not used to people refusing me. Put yourself right away to work. Find something respectable — and bring it here. Don't hide anything for yourself. If you are loyal to me — I will not abuse you.

(*Hershel gets up slowly. Silently busies himself with a corpse. He removes a wristwatch from a corpse and hands it over to Wolf*)

Wolf: Now I like you, now take from him the clothes for yourself.

(*Hershel begins to remove the coat and suddenly cries out*)

Wolf: What is it? What happened?

Hershel: He's alive! He moved?

Wolf: Oh — you are a coward!

Hershel: Listen; he groaned

(W*olf comes closer to them*)

Wolf: Yes, he's moving.

Hershel: Something has to be done with him.

Wolf: How will you help him? Let's take a look first, see what happened to him

(*Lights a match, illuminating the man*)

Hershel: God! — My brother!

(He f*alls on the ground and shakes him with all his power*) Leibel! Get up — Leibel!

Wolf: Let's carry him to the opening. It's more lit there and he'll have more air to breathe.

(*They both carry him to the opening*)

Hershel: He opened his eyes! He's looking at me! Don't you recognize me? I… I…

Leib: Hershel?... Hershel…

Hershel: It's me yes, it's me!

Leib: A drink…

Hershel: (*Desperate*) There is none, there is none…. What is the matter with you? What hurts?

Leib: Gassed…

Hershel: You've been lying here a long time?

Leib: I don't know, I lost my sense…

Wolf: (*Takes him away to the side*) you did him harm by reviving him.

Hershel: Harm? Why?

Wolf: Why does he need to die for a second time?

Hershel: He shall live!

Wolf: Empty words! If he had the proper help — possibly, but here he will die.

Leib: Hershel…

Hershel: I'm here.

Leib: How does it look in the ghetto?

Hershel: The Germans are moving from house to house, sweeping up the whole ghetto.

Leib: And what will happen to you?

Hershel: Why are you concerned about me? I am healthy, and you… How did you get gassed? You really went through the sewer.

Leib: There were a lot of us… The opening to the sewer — very small… I let in other ones first… By the time it was my turn I was already gassed… But you live, so I can die in peace…

Hershel: You will not die! You will recover and come with us!

Wolf: We must set out on the road soon. Staying here longer is very Dangerous.

Leib: The friend is right.

Hershel: I will carry you on my back.

Leib: Hershel, this is above your capabilities.

Hershel: I will stay with you.

Leib: You shouldn't. You will not help me with it, and you will die too. Don't be stubborn. You always used to obey me. Obey me for the last time. And to you, friend, I have a request; do you possibly have a revolver?

Wolf: I do.

Leib: And bullets?

Wolf: Only two bullets

Leib: Could you spare one for me?

Wolf: What do you need a bullet for?

Leib: To kill myself.

Hershel: Oh God! What are you saying?!

Leib: I could be suffering here for another day or two. Better — all at once.

Wolf: I understand you. But this is not up to me.

Leib: Then up to whom?

Wolf: Up to your brother. He has to agree to give you his bullet.

Leib: What do you mean by that?

Wolf: I have two bullets. If we are in danger of falling into German hands, it's one bullet for him — and one for me.

Leib: Hershel give up your bullet for your brother…

Hershel: No, no, you've done so much for me —

Leib: Do it for me this time and forgive me, for taking your bullet. You're not even going to need it, you will save yourself. (*To Wolf*) *you* will do it. I am too weak. I may not be able to do it in one shot and may need another. I will not take your bullet as well.

Wolf: I will do it.

(*Hershel Breaks out crying*)

Leib: And one more request for you: don't do it in front of his eyes but above. Carry me up through the rubble. I do not want to lie in a cellar, in the wetness and darkness, Let the rats eat me.

Wolf: I will do like you ordered.

Leib: So take me… You should free yourself from me, the sooner the better, you should think about yourselves.

Hershel: I will not allow… No!

Leib: You are still a child. We are both older than you are, and know better. Take care!

(W*olf picks up Leib and carries him up. A moment goes by and a shot is heard. Hershel screams, after that a lamentable cry.* W*olf is back*)

Wolf: Calm down, Hershel…

Hershel: And I let it all happen!

Wolf: Saving him was already not possible anyway. He might have lived for another day or two, and suffered. I saved him from suffering. I liked him, that brother of yours. I really was a smuggler, but I have respect for him. He struggled, sacrificed himself for others, and died bravely.

Hershel: Now I am alone, all alone in this world…

Wolf: You are not alone. I am with you. I will take your brother's place. I will take care of you in his place. And, if God forbid, the Germans catch us, I will give you, if you want — the second bullet — my own… I'll do it all for you…

End

The same Fate

(*Evening time at home. Mother is sitting at the table knitting a sweater. There is knocking on the door*)

Mother: Who is it? Who's knocking?

A voice: Open! It's me.

Mother: Oh God! It really is father!

(*For a moment she remains standing frozen, a clapping is heard again. She opens the door. Father shows up.*)

Papa, did you really come to us?

(*Hugs and kisses him*)

You shouldn't walk around that late at night. You could get shot!

Grandpa: (*Caressing her hair*) Well, good, good — calm yourself down.

Mother: I haven't seen you in such a long time!

Grandpa: And your mother you have seen, ah? Well, have no fear, I know that she used to come to you in secret and even stayed around.

Mother: You really finally came.

Grandpa: I haven't changed, but the times have. If I once couldn't force you to be Jewish — now the Germans are doing it. We'll have to reckon with them soon.

Mother: I never left the Jewish people.

Grandpa: But you took a gentile for a husband.

Mother: Shall people always fight with one another?

Grandpa: The prophet Isaiah spoke about the future — about the end of days, when a lion and a lamb will feed peacefully. An animal with an animal — yes, and a man with a man not? Surely men must start sometime, but the way I see it, to begin with peace would require the lion to start, not the lamb.

Mother: And indeed my husband started that with me.

Grandpa: Just wait: and that child of yours, what is he?

Mother: What is that child? — A man.

Grandpa: You are mistaken. There is no such thing. If he's not a Jew, then, when in such an environment — he is a gentile.

Mother: And do you think that I have really been away from the Jewish people?

Grandpa: You cannot tear yourself entirely from the Jewish people and be estranged from it, because I'm your father, because your childhood reminds you a lot of Jewish things. A Jewish word, a Jewish holiday, a Jewish custom — but your child, what will he remember?

Mother: I, nevertheless, am afraid that this child will have something to remember. Not remembering his Jewish heritage, like us, but the days of misfortune and pain.

Grandpa: I have very sad news for you. You must know the whole truth. A Jew came running in here from the shtetl of Skala. He says that the Germans have assembled all the Jews in the cemetery, ordered them to dig graves and then — listen to what they went through! — Shot with machineguns. Only that Jew alone managed by a miracle to save himself and run here.

Mother: And here he is safe?

Grandpa: Sure, who knows what can still happen here. Yes daughter, don't think that I came here to argue with you or to moralize. I came here for something very different. I have to tell you openly: it was hard, it was very hard for me to come to you, but your mother had exhausted me. Go, see — she said — how she's doing. Her husband isn't there. The Germans took him away, and who knows what happened to him. She lives among gentile neighbors, but she really is Jewish, like all of us.

Mother: My dear mother!

Grandpa: I came to see how you manage and also because of something else: so that you'll come over to us with the child. Among Jews you will feel after all, more at home.

Mother: I thank you Papa. I thought that you would never forgive me. But isn't it already difficult enough for you to make ends meet for you, to now have me too?

Grandpa: Daughter, whatever we cook, we can peel a few more potatoes. Anyway I'm not promising you any roasted birds. What we'll eat, you and your child will eat.

(*Someone knocking on the door*)

Mother: Who could be knocking so late? Should I open?

Grandpa: For small crimes, once a lock and key were enough. Now, there is no defense. Better to open.

(*She goes to the door*)

Mother: No, papa, I will go open the door. With you it is plain to see that you are a Jew. Go into the next room.

Grandpa: So be it, like you say.

(*Goes into the second room, she goes to open the door. A neighbor comes in*)

Neighbor: Good evening.

Mother: Good evening. Is that you? — So late? What's happening?

Neighbor: Nothing unusual. I wouldn't have come at all, but my wife — you understand…

Mother: I don't understand at all, what do you actually want?

Neighbor: My wife, that is, my wife's sister, she has a groom, the groom is a policeman, today he told my wife's sister, that tomorrow the Jews are going to be led to the cemetery and there —

Mother: All, be killed.

Neighbor: No, what are you saying? From there they will be sent to various work places.

Mother: This is the official version, but do you know what happened with the Jews of the Skala shtetl?

Neighbor: I do not know.

Mother: They were tricked into the cemetery, and killed there. Did you really not know about it? But what does it have to do with your visit?

Neighbor: You see, if tomorrow you pull out of here, the dwelling is vacant — my wife told me, I should go to you… we have a small apartment…

Mother: That means that you are already prepared to take over our apartment. Very nice. It makes me happy to see my inheritors. But must you hurry up, and, already at night? Don't you have any patience to wait till the morning, when we're all away from here?

Neighbor: Then others could come.

Mother: You want to seize the opportunity, aha…

Neighbor: Don't think it is only for our own good. Some unknown people could come from the street and take everything. Then your belonging will be lost forever. With us — when you come back, you'll have your things back.

Mother: I think you can relax, we're not coming back.

Neighbor: But one can never know —

Mother: So what do you exactly want from me?

Neighbor: The keys for the door and the closet…

Mother: (*Looks at him frozen for a moment*) Good, I will give them to you.

Neighbor: I see that you are an outstanding woman.

Mother: This is still not everything. I can take certain things with me, but I will take nothing. I will leave everything to you.

Neighbor: This is very nice on your part. I thank you!

Mother: But I'm asking for something for it.

Neighbor: What do you want then?

Mother: My child should stay with you.

Neighbor: Hmmm… This is not a small thing.

Mother: His father was really Polish.

Neighbor: But his mother Jewish… And you do really know that concealing a Jew is dangerous.

Mother: At first you will have to hide him, but as soon as the days of panic are over, you should not have any fear. Look, I'm giving you this wristwatch of mine (*does that*) I'm giving you all my money (*Takes out money from her handbag and lays it down*) here are some gold and silverwares. (*Takes them out of the closet*) I also have butter (*takes it out of the closet*) All of this you can take, and I'm prepared to give it to you if you will hide my child.

Neighbor: (*Looks at every object with greed, and finally says*) Good. You really understand… This child will have to be nourished, he'll need clothes, shoes, to boot, you really need…

Mother: I thank you — you can take it all, it's yours.

(*He pounces right away on the things, he puts them in a pouch that he pulls out of his pocket and packs it together hastily*)

Mother: And when will you pick up the child?

Neighbor: The child?... where is the child then?

Mother: He lies asleep in the next room.

Neighbor: Well, good; you will wake up the child, get him ready, and meanwhile I'll take the things to my place. Besides, I have to talk about it with my wife.

Mother: Oh, now you have to talk with your wife about it?... well, go, talk with her and come back soon.

Neighbor: When you are ready with the child, knock on the wall. I will hear and come right in.

(*She remains standing for a while, thinking, finally she says*)

Mother: And now, to wake up the child, and get him ready.

(*Goes into the room on the left where the child is sleeping, the door on the right opens, and her father is at the threshold. She pulls him in.*)

Oh, papa, you must stay here with me for the night. If you go now into the street you can still get shot.

Grandpa: Apparently we're all destined to die.

Mother: What? You heard our talk?

Grandpa: Even though the door was closed, some sound went through it.

Mother: I will give him the child.

Grandpa: Not good, daughter.

Mother: Do you know the responsibility I have? It is my child.

Grandpa: And you are my child.

Mother: Does the person who gave life to this child, also has the right to give him death?

Grandpa: No. But that said person has to answer for this life. For raising it, and you want to give it to someone else.

Mother: This is not my concern. For me it is enough that my child will live.

Grandpa: Daughter! In the morning we are going to our deaths. Your husband was arrested as a communist. Since the Germans went into the city there hasn't been any sign of life from him. This child will stay with them. And what is a child? — A child is a continuation of you, of me, of our people, of our customs and language. From all of it, this child will be torn away and estranged. It will be a statement against all of which we died for, and also against all that we suffered so much for.

Mother: Should I lead him to death by myself? Seeing with my own eyes, how a bullet makes a hole in his golden head, or how they'll burry him alive? His body that I have watched over with a shudder, so that it may not get cold or pricked; all of a sudden abandon it into the murderous hands? No, I cannot allow it. No mother in the world can allow it!

Grandpa: And for me it is hardest of all to bear that this child will die, while being a Jew, and knowing nothing of Judaism.

Mother: I think I heard steps in the child's room. Did he wake from his sleep?

(*She goes to the door that leads to the bedroom on the left, opens it cautiously, and remains standing at the threshold*)

— What is the matter with you? I thought, that you went to sleep long ago, but you are walking around the room.

Child: I cannot sleep.

(*She leads him to her, and looks him over*)

Mother: What's happened? Why is your face so pale?

(*Brings him under the light, his shirt is unbuttoned*)

Blue marks on your chest!

(*Removing his shirt*)

And the shoulders are wounded! How did this happen?! When?!

Child: Earlier during the day

Mother: During the day? And you kept quiet this whole time and told me nothing!

Child: It didn't hurt so much before. Now I cannot lie in bed.

Mother: And who is the bad person who did it to you?

Child: Kajik.

Mother: Who is Kajik?

Child: Well, you really know him — the tall one, the neighbor's son.

Mother: (W*ith horror*) what are you saying? The neighbor's child! And why did he hit you — did you throw a rock at him?

Child: No.

Mother: And didn't take a toy away from him?

Child: Also not.

Mother: Than why did he hit you? Just like that? — I can't believe it. Tell me how it happened.

Child: Today when I went out to the street, he was standing there with other children. He turns to me and yells: Zjidzje!*

Mother: And what did you answer?

---

* Jew/ (Derogatory/Polish)

Child: I said to him: Drongal.

Mother: Why of all things?

Child: That's what they call him, because he's tall… So he jumped on me and beat me… he's stronger…

Mother: Well, and the friends, what did they do?

Child: They laughed, and when Kajik left me and I ran home, they yelled: "Zjidzje" one even threw a rock after me.

Mother: You should not have called him Drongal.

Child: And why he was allowed to call me Zjidzje?

(*Her father who was standing in the background, approaches the child*)

Grandpa: And do you think that being a Jew is shameful?

Child: (Looks at *him* in wonderment) who is he mamashy?

Mother: This is your grandfather, my child.

Child: He looks like the holy Mikolay!

Grandpa: No, I'm not holy Mikolay. I'm a simple Jew.

Child: You are a Jew? And you are really my Grandpa for real?

Mother: Yes, Yanek, this is my father.

Child: And the Bobeshy* that comes to us, so goody, always kisses me and brings me candy — she is also Jewish?

Grandpa: Yes. She is Jewish, and your mama, and I.

Child: Everybody Jewish?

Grandpa: Everybody.

Mother: Father, this isn't the time, he should be getting ready.

Grandpa: And you still think the same?

Mother: I must, I must. No other choice. Listen Yanek, we — we are going away, we need to leave tomorrow. I want you to go until we're back, to the neighbor, to Mr. Vladislav.

Child: No, no, I will not go. Kajik will yell at me Zjidzje again, and beat me!

Mother: My God, what do I do?

Grandpa: He is a Jew, and our fate is also his.

Mother: Don't talk like that. I will not ask this child. (*Runs to the wall and begins to bang on it*) Let him come and take him. I will force this child to go. He must go! Yanek come here, I will dress you up.

Child: (*Runs to his grandfather*) Grampa, tell mama not to make me go,

(*clings to him*)

---

*Endearing word for Bobeh/ Grandma

Grandpa: Daughter you hear? Let him be until the neighbor will pick him up from here.

Mother: So what do you want to do?

Grandpa: You will see soon. Yanek, does it still hurt?

Child: Still a little bit.

Grandpa: Would you like me to tell you a story?

Child: Oy tell me, tell me!

Grandpa: So listen: once upon a time in a far, far away land, lived a man, and his name was Abraham.

Child: (*repeats slowly, as if he would try to remember or recall something*) Ab-ra-ham…

Grandpa: And the said Abraham had a son, and only one, and his name was Isaac.

Child: Is-aac

Grandpa: Once God — have you seen the blue heaven and the pretty stars in it at night? There he lives, the God of Abraham — once told him: take your son, your only one, the one you love — Isaac, and sacrifice him to me.

Mother: And the neighbor isn't coming.

Grandpa: Maybe he didn't hear you knocking?

Mother: This is not possible. If someone puts a nail in the wall on the other side, I always hear it.

Grandpa: He's probably dealing with his wife, and the wife does not consent, or she's just afraid.

Mother: My God, this cannot happen! I'll keep on trying.

(*Bangs harder on the wall*)

Child: Grampa, why did you stop the story?

Grandpa: Ah, Where was I?

Child: And God said to Abraham…

Grandpa: Yes, and God said to Abraham, take your son, your only one, that you love, Isaac, and sacrifice him to me.

Child: And what such thing is a sacrifice?

Grandpa: It's a sign of loyalty and submission. So Abraham woke up early, saddled his donkey and went with Isaac on the road. They advanced farther and farther, until they came to a mountain. On the mountain Abraham lay down the wood and on the pile of wood, he tied Isaac. Isaac asked: papa, what are you doing? And Abraham answered: I want to bring you to God as a sacrifice. And do you love your God? Asked Isaac, and Abraham answered: I love him very much. So bring me to him as a sacrifice, said Isaac. Abraham lifted the knife, but his hand was shaking. Isaac saw it and said to his father: papa, still yourself!

Child: Oy, how brave — was Isaac!

Grandpa: Abraham lifts the knife, but suddenly he fills how someone stops the hand with the knife. And he sees — an angel! Ah, how do you like Isaac?

Child: Oh-oh, a lot!

Grandpa: And you too, would not have feared the knife?

Child: I would not fear, and anyway, I know that the angel will come and stop the hand with the knife…

Grandpa: My child, the angel doesn't always come…

Mother: And the neighbor is not coming. He's not coming!

(*She walks to the window. Lifts the shade, into the room comes a gush of morning light.*)

— Woe is me, it is already day time!

(*From the street a drumming is being heard. The drumming is coming closer. The drumming stops and someone is announcing*)

Voice: In order of the city commander! This morning, all Jews must gather at the cemetery. Whoever will not come out and hide will be shot on site wherever found!

(*The drumming starts again, and then slowly fades away*)

Mother: Father, Yanek, we will go. (*To the child*) I just now finished knitting a sweater. Take it, put it on, so that you won't be cold on the road.

Child: (*Happy*) I will take it with me, will I really go together with you?

Mother: Yes, my child, you will go together with us.

(*She dresses up the child with the sweater. And holds his hand*)

Grandpa: And the angel didn't come…

Child: Where are we going mama?

Mother: Far, my child, far away from here.

Child: And if father will come looking for us, how will he find us?

Mother: Child of mine, if father will come back, he will not find us here. But he'll find our enemies and will take revenge for us, revenge!

End

Other one act plays

A watch

He: I bought myself a watch. It is quite a watch. It is by no means an alarm clock, it lets me sleep as much as I like. It is also no wristwatch – I do not look at it at lunch time or in the evening, when I ought to have supper. The watch is for me a shield. When I am hungry – I eat. What sort of a watch is this you ask? – This is a singular one – a strange one. Each time it hears a lie – it rings. I go into a store of a good friend and he assures me that he's selling to me especially cheap – the watch rings. When I go through the garden and see how a couple sits embracing on a bench and he avows to her his eternal love, the watch rings. But the watch rings the most when I go to meetings at the congregation or to a bank. It rings and rings and won't stop. I fear to take it there. But here, to the theater I do bring it. I shouldn't fear, because I know it sees the very best and good looking audience in the world. (*The watch rings*) And you know, that I am the very best actor on the Jewish stage. (*The watch rings louder still*). I know that one should never go to a home or a store to sell tickets, but I come, and put it in the safe two weeks ahead of time, (*Watch rings*) and as I am an actor who doesn't, by all means mind, the four pesos for a
ticket, but only would want to procure happiness and laughter *(watch rings)*. It seems… that it rang; probably there is a church nearby…

Not only am I a great actor, but also an intelligent man: I read the newspapers every day. I want to understand politics. I want to make contemporaneous jokes, not about mothers-in-law and wives who fool men whenever they can. I always carry with me a bunch of newspapers, so that I can live with the times. If you'd like, I will indeed, read to you some news of world politics. Here is the first news item: Molotov, made a declaration, that the Soviet Union only thinks of peace (t*he watch rings*). That Russia does not intend to take over foreign lands (The watch rings) the best evidence is that Russia took over Poland, Rumania, Czechoslovakia, Bulgaria, Lithuania, Latvia and Estonia. And England wants war, the evidence is – that they gave up India, Palestine, the Suez Canal… That in Russia, the worker has enough (*watch rings*). What are you ringing for you foolish watch? Surely the worker there has enough. He's got enough Molotov, enough Khrushchev, and he's got more than enough five year plans and Kolkhozes…

Or now I will read to you about a recent reception here, in honor of a distinguished social activist on his travel to Europe and Israel. Here I read: he has been all of his life a devoted worker. He had not, in a sense, been engaged in his own business, but strove to serve the Jewish masses. (*watch rings*). He has always been a modest man and never endeavored to become president, secretary, or even a member of a committee (*watch rings*). He has always been the first to donate to the Magbit foundation, and to the Jewish National Fund (w*atch rings*). Now he is going on a journey, to get acquainted with the conditions in Israel while he will relinquish all his business and will permanently settle on the land (*watch rings*). All the speakers at the reception have praised him and practically wept for having to separate from him, as he has in Buenos Aires, only friends. (*Watch rings).*

Maybe I should let go of politics and chronicles of social life, and simply read to you some Avisas, that is the announcements. (*Reads*) "A young woman looking for a man" Since the announcement comes under the heading of 'For rent', it looks like the editor was mistaken. Let us now read under the rubric "Passing over" It looks, on further inspection 'A girl 37 years of age (*the watch rings*) looking for a man up to forty. Nice. (*Watch rings*) modest, (*watch rings*) loyal, (*watch rings*) but with no money. To tell you the truth: I like her. She probably has to be a respectable girl. That she has no money – doesn't play any role. I am ready to meet with her and possibly marry her (*watch rings*) it seems that something is ringing… I must have caught a cold, my ears are ringing. (*Takes out cotton*) one has to fill them in… (*Does that* and *a girl shows up*) Good evening miss, would you possibly know where the street… the street named… I forgot what exactly the name of that street was.

She: You have some nerve bothering me, I am not used to this type of thing… (*watch rings*)

He: Forgive me miss, I am a stranger here… Do not know anyone… (*watch rings*)

She: If you hadn't interrupted me now in the street that late, I would have already been where I was supposed to be. This is the first time in my life, that I am out in the street that late without my mother (*watch rings*). I am leaving now from a friend. She lies in the hospital… she is in labor… Oy is this painful…

He: I must confess for myself that I had never been in labor… but as you say, miss, that it is very painful probably you of all people know it… or you wouldn't just say that…

She: Do not indulge in it too much sir. I do not understand such things. I only occupy myself with spiritual things (*watch rings*). I only look at a man's soul. (*watch rings*)

He: We are really alike: I too, only look at a woman's soul (*hugs her*)

She: Except that. That I don't like. (*Watch rings*)

He: So give me a kiss. Just one kiss. I assure you, that for me it is only a spiritual thing. Oy, if I could only kiss your soul without you. (*Watch rings*) but this is not possible. (*gives her a kiss. She is startled*) see how startled you are. The soul is at the tip of your nose. Allow me to kiss your soul.

(Kisses the tip of her nose)

She: You are not allowed to kiss.

He: Why not?

She: Because mother said not to. Mother, as a young girl, also never kissed… (*watch rings*) What are you thinking about now?

He: Same as you.

She: Fey, you ought to be ashamed…

He: I can no longer take it, I must kiss your soul. (*Kisses her*)

She: (*Tears herself away from him*)

How dare you do it? How dare you bother an innocent girl who lives in 3861 Lavelle Street on the second floor, Apartment A, where one can find her there from 11 o'clock till the morning?

He: *(Looks for a pen and cannot find one*) won't you by any chance, have a pen? I want to write it down.

She: Men like that everything will be given to them… even a pen… take it and write away. *(Gives him a pen)*

He: And suppose there had been a plan for me to go straight to your place? I remember an address after being there just once.

She: What are you saying? No man had ever crossed the threshold of my room (*watch rings*) I will go home now and do some reading.

He: What do you plan to read?

She: I now read – the Bible in Spanish. (*Watch rings*) I am at the point of reading how the three guests came to Sarah and told her that in a year she will have a child.

He: This happened once… But today guests come – and there are no children… I have an idea… Let's get together and read the bible (*watch rings*)

She: You know, it is such an old bible that is worth possibly a million…

He: I love a young bible…

She: I also like to knit a sweater… (*watch rings*). You will sit and see how I knit, how I darn socks… (*watch rings*) What is that ringing coming from you all the time?

He: It is a watch, each time it hears a lie – it rings.

She: (*Upset*) And with such a watch you want to come to a woman? And I thought, that you were serious. Fey, shame on you, shame on you. (*Runs away*).

The bad omen

(The table is set. Anna is standing by the mirror. She is dressing up, as if for a holiday)

Anna: *(To the mirror)* When I am old, I will probably look like a…

(She imitates an old grandmother)

Oy, Oy, my lower back. (With a different tone) Where are you my husband? Would you direct to me the fire-pot, to chase away the cold? Hand over the stick – I must lean on it, for the legs can no longer carry me. *(Pause)* Praise to God, it is still holding. A man must go on living. As my mamaleh says: the more man lives the more he wants to. My dear mama, it's a shame she is not with us today. Exactly today when I would like that she would be with Bernard and me. Today, when it is a year since Bernard and I were married.

(*Bernard appears*)

Bernard: I have brought you flowers, my dear. I saw them in the street and brought them here, so they should see what a pretty wife I have. They should also see how we celebrate our one year anniversary, and especially at home and especially without a hullabaloo. Well, give me a kiss, and give me some food, my heart is falling out.

Anna: One really needs to respond with something to your speech, but I don't know with what. Shush, I already know. I will stand on a stool. *(Does that*) Distinguished husband of mine, it is for me a great honor to have such

a good and wise husband for a – husband… *(both laugh)*
And it gives me great pleasure, that my husband's little wife is, too, not a foolish wife and now I will call out loud: long live the thirteen of May. (*Taken aback*) Oy vey to me, the thirteen…

Bernard: What is, the thirteen?

Anna: How can you ask? Thirteen, really is a bad number.

Bernard: How do you know that?

Anna: The entire world knows that, and you act stupid.

Bernard: There is no limit to what the world knows and what the world thinks. Now the world thinks that the president of the congregation, or of the DAIA* or the world congress is a great man… That the newspapers' editors tell the truth… That the bank directors only lose their own money… That having money, means being rich… That to be a progressive – one must be a worker… Enough, let's leave the world alone and go to the table. Ha, where is our servant?

Anna: I sent her home. I wanted for us to be alone, entirely alone. I even prepared the meal by myself. And if it doesn't taste good to you – you have no choice and just the same you must say that you like it. The soup will be a little cold, therefore the compote will be a little warm. The meat will be too hard, therefore the ice-cream will be soft and flowing like water. Ay, I believe…

* Organization representing the Jews in Argentina

Bernard: I do not believe in any omens. I do not even believe in the legend about bad mothers in law. A mother in law is, after all, also a mother, a wife, a sister, a child, a loved one, but people talk about mothers in law – they make them out to be witches with whiskers and moles on their faces.

Anna: You want to insult my mother? My mother has on her face –

Bernard: *(Wants to take it back)* these are not moles, these are raisins. Raisins and almonds…

Anna: (*When she's busy at the table, she drops a knife*) Oy vey to me.

Bernard: What is it?

Anna: I dropped the knife.

Bernard: A new misfortune for the Jews – she dropped a knife. (*Picks it up*) Here I picked it up and no more misfortune.

Anna: No, you don't understand. That doesn't help. I fear that we must have a fight.

Bernard: Rea—lly? We must? Who will force us? The AMIA?* the DAIA?

Anna: You laugh, but for me it is not a laughing matter. The last thing we need is, God forbid, to have a fight today, today when it is our wedding anniversary, exactly on the thirteen…

---

* Jewish community center in Buenos Aires

Bernard: If it wasn't unfortunate to have a wedding on the thirteen, it is certainly not unfortunate to celebrate the one year anniversary on the thirteen.

Anna: You start again? You talk about the thirteen? – I am only talking about the knife.

Bernard: What now with the knife? Another nonsense? Another superstition?

Anna: (*All serious*) this is not at all a superstition, my dear. Everybody knows, that if they drop a knife while eating, then they have to fight.

Bernard: So-ooo? Everybody knows? So I am part of the world and I do not know of it. I'm hearing it for the first time.

Anna: And you call yourself an intelligent man? And you further say that you studied in a university? Every silly thing you learned there, and about that, they forgot to tell you!

Bernard: And I am telling you again, that this was invented by savage people.

Anna: Is my mother now a savage person?

Bernard: I didn't say that, now, did I?

Anna: You said it, said it. Because I heard it from my dear mama's mouth. What are you going to say now?

Bernard: What could I say? I only say that I should have horns, if I knew with what to believe, that a knife is a fortune teller. I hear this for the first time.

Anna: Again he hears it for the first time. I am still telling you, that my mother said that.

Bernard: Ay, Let's leave your mother alone. But you, are talking silly.

Anna: Who talks silly?

Bernard: Old wives.

Anna: Is now my mother an old wife? Since she dyed her hair and got false teeth, she doesn't look older than sixty.

Bernard: If so, then young wives talk silly.

Anna: Ah, that means me.

Bernard: I ask you much, not to change the subject. I am really talking about your mother.

Anna: My mother is always smarter than yours.

Bernard: Don't bring my mother into this.

Anna: What is it, your mother is imported goods, and mine was bought off a stockade? From an old railway car?

Bernard: I'm asking you again not to talk about my mother.

Anna: And if I will not do it to you, and not talk, what will you make of it that the butcher would say…

Bernard: What would the butcher say?

Anna: The butcher is not the only one. The Jew from the store, also says the same thing.

Bernard: What is the Jew from the store is now saying?

Anna: He says that, which the milkman says –

Bernard: (*With the knife in his hand*) Hear now what I am saying to you, my little wife. I very much would not like to fight with you about that filthy knife, but I must tell you, my dear wife. That if your mother drove into your head such foolishness – then one cannot consider her anything but an old farm animal.

Anna: And your mother is a thief.

Bernard: My mother a thief? I'm going to kill you. Take your life. Soon. Right away. Now.

(Chases her with the knife in his hand. She runs from him across the stage)

Bernard: (*Suddenly stops, sobers up*) Oy, forgive me. Exactly on our one year's wedding anniversary, forgive me…

Anna: Now, do you believe that when a knife falls, people must fight?

Bernard: I believe… I believe…

Anna: Was I right, or not?

Bernard: You were right…

Anna: And my mother?

Bernard: Your mother, was also right. All mothers in law in the world are right, all mothers in law…

Yiddel with a fiddle and Berl with a bass.

Yiddel: (*comes in*) this was already some wedding. The real big-shot. The golden chicken soup. The roasted hens and geese. But to a little wine this didn't come and to liquor certainly not. A father in-law complained to me: Rabbi Yiddel, food – as much as I like. But with the drinks – A little bit restrained, while you have to, of all things, play. Rabbi Zerakh – I answer – you have a badly prepared table. From drinking the feet wobble, but not the hands. On the contrary, the hands first become courageous. On the road I got a bottle. Well, show here your smart little feet. Let me give you a kiss.

(T*akes a swig from the bottle)*

And now, like it ought to be.

(Puts a glass on the table, fills it up, wants to take a sip holds it off does not drink anything alone, gets a second glass, clangs it with his own glass) L'khayim!

Berl: *(Shows up, raises the second glass and clangs Yiddel's glass)* L'khaim!

Yiddel: L'khaim – ah? Then who are you?

Berl: You already don't recognize me? The nose is shielding your eyes?

Yiddel: It looks to me like bah- bah- bah- bah…

Berl: Don't bahbah. It is me Berl with the bass.

Yiddel: What is this L'khaim about, when with you, it is to death. As you've been already dead for a Year.

Berl: Who dead? What dead? When a klezmer sees a little liquor – he comes out of the dead – alive!

Yiddel: Nevertheless I am a little scared. If you are alive – one should go and bring the good news – to your wife, so that she would come here.

Berl: Ay you bandit! Now you want *me* to be scared.

Yiddel: How did you travel here from the netherworld?

Berl: Not long ago it was Simkhat-Torah. I played and played for a whole day.

Yiddel: What kind of a celebration is for them Simkhat-Torah in heaven, that the Torah they gave us is, of all places, here upon the earth.

Berl: Indeed for that. Since the Jews received it, they have been breathing easier in heaven. And the Jews have had to bear a terrible sorrow…

Yiddel: What does Simkhat-Torah have to do with your coming here?

Berl: It is related. I was playing and playing a whole day, but the creator wanted more and more. I Already had callouses on my fingers and he still wanted me to play more. I put the bass away and say: basta. Falls to me the master of the universe: A little bit more, and I will pay

you with…
With what I ask, and feel that I can have it my way. I will make you, says he, the governor of the first heaven. No, I respond, I do not want to. So he says: I will make you the governor of three heavens at once. No, I was being stubborn, I have the heaven on earth – I want the earth. What do you mean you want the earth? – asks the creator. I want to go down once more to earth – I respond – that is all. And why do you want that – asks me the creator. I have there a friend, Yiddel, that is, Yiddel with a fiddle. I want to see him. I want, just one more time, to play with him a tune, and just one more time to have a drink with him. Good, says the master of the universe, I will do this for you, but with one condition: I will send with you an angel. The angel of missions, Mishngod. He will accompany you. I already know from experience, that a lot of messengers do not come back… they remain upon the earth… So this is how, I returned here.

Yiddel: that means, that with you also came an angel. A real angel. I want to see him!

Berl: Some bargain – an angel. God makes such, a thousand pieces a day!

Yiddel: And how does he manage to feed them?

Berl: Do they eat? – Angels don't eat.

Yiddel: And what kind of a trick is that? If my children didn't have to eat – they too would be angels.

Berl: In heaven I am sad. I cannot take it.

Yiddel: I don't understand why it's bad for you. You of all people live from playing, from art.

Berl: I indeed live from art. But I have great trouble with the angels

Yiddel: What kind of trouble?

Berl: They loaf around idle the whole day. They do not want to learn to read music. They do not even know who Beethoven was, they don't have to learn, they say, because they are angels.

Angel: (*Calls from behind the scene*) Berl, Berl! It's already time for you to return to heaven.

Yiddel: Call in the angel. I am dying to see him.

Berl: Die, and then you will.

Yiddel: And now, it is not possible?

Berl: Since we are good brothers, I will do that for you. I will call him in. *(calls)* Rabbi Missiongod, please excuse us and come here for a moment!

(*An angel appears. Older. Speaks with a twang)*

Angel: What are you doing here Berl? What is this water in a little glass?

Berl: Liquor

Angel: Liquor? – Don't mock me you impudent!

Berl: It is a kind of refreshment. Such drink does not exist in heaven, you know.

Angel: And our preserved wine?

Berl: Inappropriate example! There is no comparison!

Angel: And the water from the rivers of heaven? – From the Tigris? The Euphrates and Pishon?

Berl: Try it for yourself, you will soon taste the real flavor. A heavenly flavor!

Yiddel: Taste a little.

Angel: Well, one shouldn't

Berl: Try, and soon you would.

(Pours him a small glass)

Angel: Just one sip, nothing more!

(Takes a sip and begins to cough)

Oy, how it burns. This is not water but fire!

Yiddel: Drink a little more. Indulge yourself.

(The angel drinks some more)

Angel: Oy, I can no longer stand on my feet!

Yiddel: But what do you need feet for? To stand on the ground? You have wings.

Angel: My head is swinging. I must rest a little.

(Lies down on the couch)

Yiddel: I had no idea, that your angels had such weak heads.

Berl: As you can see – in there – I don't lick any honey.

Yiddel: And to be that close to the stars and clouds, is nothing for you?

Berl: A fiddle is light, you can fly with it where you want, but a bass is heavy, one must stand and rest it on the ground. Therefore I miss the earth.

Yiddel: And if there was a plan to make a switch?

Berl: With what? With the instruments?

Yiddel: No, with the worlds! You should stay here, and I will go to heaven in your place.

Berl: I accept! But what will the angel say?

Yiddel: He is drunk. He will not notice. We will exchange our clothes.

Berl: And what will the Lord say?

Yiddel: Why would *he* complain? What band would not be happy to receive for a bass – a fiddle? And moreover for the same price!

Berl: It is done.
(They exchange their clothes while singing)

This old familiar song
Now it will be changed
Berl will soon be Yiddel
And Yiddel will be Berl.

Now sing this song like this
In the home and in the street
Berl – with a fiddle
And Yiddel with a bass.

Yiddel: Now go wake the angel. I will just grab my fiddle and go with him.

Berl: Call that fiddle – La Fidalty! One should not take with him anything from the other world.

Yiddel: If so – The exchange is no exchange.

Berl: Changing your mind, is not acceptable, such a thing is not allowed! You must go!

Yiddel: And I'm telling you again that I will not go!

Berl: *(wakes up the angel)* Rabbi Missiongod, get up and take your guest with you!

Angel: *(takes Yiddel for Berl. To Yiddel):*
Come on, It's late!

Yiddel: I am not going!

Angel: Oh – wow! A mutiny! You will not come?! IF you come willingly, you will fly up on my soft feathers and it will be soft and warm. But if you will not go willingly – the devil will carry you up. He will grab you with the sharp and pointy fingernails of his hands. He will bite you, he will tear you!

Yiddel: No – no! Without the fiddle I will not go even into heaven! Not even into the Garden of Eden! No – no!

(There is more light now. He wakes up. Looks around)

Where am I? In this world or in the hereafter? – Soon I will find out: the fiddle hangs on the wall?
— Yes. First sign. The bottle of liquor is on the table? – Yes. Second sign. And now to sign number three:

(Calling out loudly)

Sarah-Trayneh! Sarah-Trayneh!

(A voice is heard from behind the scene)

You already came? Schlimazel! Nuisance! convulsions for you! Violent death!

Yiddel: Yes! Yes! I am of this world! Of this world…

End

89028010R00174

Made in the USA
Columbia, SC
16 February 2018